The Four Vision Quests of Jesus

STEVEN CHARLESTON

Morehouse Publishing
NEW YORK

Unless otherwise noted, the Scripture quotations contained herein are from the New Revised Standard Version Bible, copyright © 1989 by the Division of Christian Education of the National Council of Churches of Christ in the U.S.A. Used by permission.
All rights reserved.

Morehouse Publishing, 19 East 34th Street, New York, NY 10016

Morehouse Publishing is an imprint of Church Publishing Incorporated.

www.churchpublishing.org

Cover design by Laurie Klein Westhafer

Typeset by Denise Hoff

Library of Congress Cataloging-in-Publication Data

A catalog record of this book is available from the Library of Congress.

Printed in the United States of America

To Susan

Contents

THE CIRCLE

My family has lived in America for thirty thousand years.[1] They farmed the land. They built towns and raised families. They worshipped God. Year after year, generation after generation, they lived in this land and they called it home.

And, yet, I am a second generation American.

When my father was born in 1923 he was not an American citizen. American Indians were not allowed to be citizens until 1924. When they thought we were all but extinct, the federal government gave us citizenship. They had done everything they could to erase our thirty thousand year history. In the end, before we disappeared forever, they wanted us to be able to be called what they called themselves: Americans. The irony of their own actions escaped them.

I share this story to welcome you into the circle of my family. I hope it will help you begin to feel a part of our story, part of the experience of our culture, our history, and our faith. If you are not a Native person by background, this way of seeing and thinking may be different for you. It may even be difficult. But however much of a challenge it may be for you to enter into the Native story, to our way of thinking and remembering, I hope you will always feel welcome in the circle of my family. You do not have to embrace everything at once. It is enough that you are here. In fact, you honor my ancestors by being here.

This book is a personal theology. It arises from my experience as both a Native American and a Christian. It is about my struggle to reconcile these two halves of who I am. I do not share this personal theology with any pretense that I am speaking for all Native people or for any other Christians. I only offer it for what it is worth as my testimony.

My book is about the four vision quests of Jesus. It tells how I came to read and interpret the Bible through the eyes of traditional Native American religion. It offers a Christian theology that is based on Native tradition, on the original Covenant God made with my ancestors, with the Native people of this continent. Therefore, my book is about the Native traditions of North America and how they are a living Covenant that can enrich and change how we understand Jesus. To help you feel welcome in this new circle of thinking, let me say a few words about how my book is put together.

First, I know that there are many different ways to refer to the indigenous people of North America. We have been called American Indians, Native Americans, and First Nations. I have used the term Native American because it seems the most common usage at the time of this writing. I also refer to what are sometimes called "tribes" as "nations" because I want to underscore the reality that Native communities were and are sovereign nations. The only time I use "tribe" is when I speak of the tribe of the human beings, an image of the human family around the world.

My book is divided into eight chapters. In the first four chapters, I consider what it means to be a spiritual seeker from the Native American viewpoint.

In chapter one, "The Quest," I ask what it means to go on a spiritual quest. In chapter two, "The Vision," I discuss the nature of sacred vision. In chapter three, "The Voice," I explore the message we receive in a vision. In chapter four, "The Messiah," I suggest how this visionary process embodies the holy.

Chapter five is a hinge chapter, "The Clown." It shifts from the broader topics about a vision quest to the more specific issues of translating those Native American understandings into a Christian theology. This chapter is a bridge between tradition and testament. Therefore, it is about John the Baptist.

The last four chapters of my book discuss the four vision quests of Jesus: "The Wilderness," "The Mountain," "The Garden," and

"The Cross." Each of these stories is taken directly from the gospel of Matthew. I use only one translation of the Bible throughout the book, the New International Version (NIV) published by Zondervan. I would recommend that you read each story as it appears in the scripture before reading the chapter: (a) Matthew 4:1–11, (b) Matthew 17:1–8, (c) Matthew 26:36–46, and (d) Matthew 27:32–55.

Matthew is the only scriptural reference I use, with a few exceptions. This keeps the focus of my theology very consistent to one gospel writer. Each one of Matthew's four vision quest stories appears within a context of Native history and culture. These contexts vary as I have tried to use the wisdom of different Native communities to articulate an interpretation of Christian themes, e.g., Lakota for the Plains tradition, Choctaw for the Woodland tradition, Hopi for the Desert tradition. At the end of the book I have "endnotes" to share references I used for that chapter or to offer a brief commentary.

My goal in writing this book is to make a contribution toward the continuing development of a Native American Christian theology based on the Native Covenant, the tradition given to our people by God over 30,000 years of our spiritual evolution on this continent, a land sovereign to our nations and sacred to our people. I hope this theology will be a support to all persons seeking spiritual wisdom and reconciliation.

Thank you for reading it. Welcome to the family.

Chapter 1

THE QUEST

On a cold autumn morning in 1973 I went out onto the roof of the apartment building where I lived in Cambridge, Massachusetts, which was student housing at the seminary I attended. It was an old brick building, four or five stories high, sitting in the midst of Harvard University. I walked out onto the flat roof and looked up at the gray New England sky. Dark clouds drifted by. The city was quiet, just waking up for the start of another day.

I took a small box of cornmeal that I had bought at the local grocery store, opened it, and slowly poured it out into a circle around me. I stood in this circle and began to pray. I turned to acknowledge the four sacred directions, calling on the spirit of each one to surround me. I prayed to the Creator above me and the Earth below me to hold me in a spiritual equilibrium. I spread my arms and asked my ancestors to hear me and come to support me in any way they could. I called on the name of Jesus.

I did all of these things because I was deeply troubled. I was a young, twenty-something Native American attending a Christian seminary to become a priest. I had chosen to do so because I felt I was called by God to a religious vocation. I believed in Jesus Christ as the Son of God and I wanted to follow him. But now I was having doubts.

My doubts came from a book by Vine Deloria, Jr. called *God Is Red*.[1] Deloria, a Native American author from South Dakota, took the position that Christianity was not the religion for Native American people. Later in life, I met Vine and we became friends. I even knew his father, a very well respected Episcopal priest and Lakota elder who served the church in South Dakota. But in these early years, when his book had just come out, I only knew Vine Deloria by the words he wrote and those words shook my world.

Vine told a familiar, but painful story. He wrote about Christianity coming to the Americas as part of the colonial expansion of Europeans. He described the abuses of the Christian missionaries against the indigenous people of this hemisphere. He deconstructed many of the basic theological positions of Christianity, such as the doctrine of original sin, and argued that Native American traditional religion was far more humane and rational. He described Christianity as a deeply flawed religion. In Vine's estimation, Christianity had been largely responsible for the destruction of Native culture. It was a tool of Western imperialism. It was a sham religion forced onto Native people by a cynical and callous colonial system. In the end, he created a spiritual crossroads for Native people: choose Christianity and adopt the religion of the oppressor or choose Native tradition and stand with the oppressed.

As a much older, and hopefully wiser, person today I can look back and see that the crossroads that Vine created was artificial. It is predicated on the assumption that everything he wrote about Christianity in the Native American context was accurate, but at the time, as a young Native person just starting theological training, it was real enough to take me out onto the roof at dawn. I had never faced this dilemma before. I was raised in a Native American family from rural Oklahoma. Like Vine, I came from a family with a history of ordained service in the Christian church. My great-grandfather and my grandfather had both been ordained pastors in the Presbyterian Church.

That Christian tradition developed among my people, the Choctaw Nation, in the early 1800s.[2] The Choctaw community had invited Presbyterian missionaries to come to our nation, which in that period of American history comprised what is now Mississippi and parts of Alabama and Louisiana. These missionaries were not imposed upon us, but came in response to our invitation. The Choctaw Nation was a large, well organized sovereign nation that had a long history with Europeans. We had known the Spanish, the French, and the

English before interacting with the white people who called them-selves Americans. In fact, we had been allies of the United States, fighting alongside American soldiers in the War of 1812.

As a confident and intellectually curious people, we wanted to learn more about the religious practices of the Europeans, by what-ever name they called themselves. After considering the different denominations we began to ask Christian pastors to come into the Choctaw Nation, not only to share their religious views, but also to help us in establishing an educational system to continue our inves-tigations into Western culture and technology. Because so much of Christian theology resonated with our own religious traditions, we quickly adopted Protestantism and began building churches. The Bible was translated into Choctaw; hymns were written in Choctaw; Choctaws began leading Christian worship services. The origins of our Christian heritage, therefore, did not follow the pattern Vine described. We were not forced to accept Jesus at the point of a gun, but evolved into a Christian nation as an expression of our own cul-ture. Missionaries were not the problem for me as a Choctaw. It was, however, Vine's analysis of what happened to Native American nations, Christian or otherwise, that began to unravel my faith.

In the 1830s the Choctaw people were the first of many Native American nations to be forced to take the Trail of Tears.[3] Bullied and cheated by the American government, we were forced out of our homeland and made to take the long walk from the southern United States to Oklahoma, the sanctuary for displaced Native nations. Thousands of our people died. The white Americans we thought of as allies betrayed us. Even though we were Christians, other Christians turned to look the other way as we were despoiled. Like vultures, they swooped in to take our land.

The Trail of Tears is a bitter legacy, one shared by many Native nations whose homelands were east of the Mississippi. And yet, as a Choctaw, I had been raised to believe that our Christian faith was part of this experience. On the long walk into exile, I had been told that our Christian faith sustained us. It spoke to us about survival through an Exodus and about God's love for the dispossessed. Like the African slaves who took our place on the land in the American South, we found Christianity to be the one thing to which we could cling when the times we endured were so harsh.

When I encountered *God is Red* the memories of the Trail of Tears came back to haunt me. It planted a seed of doubt. Had my ancestors made a mistake? Had they accepted a false religion and paid the price? The story that Vine Deloria told was not something I could dismiss. In fact, it was not something I wanted to dismiss because I was so acutely aware of what had been done to my own people. The Trail of Tears is an historical memory no Choctaw will ever forget. The loss of land, culture, language, and freedom: these are the facts of life for any Native American community. Therefore, Vine's argument spoke to a truth I already knew. It was as if John the Baptist had appeared before me, calling me to wake up and smell the coffee, repent from my devotion to the conqueror's faith, and return to the ancient heritage of a pre-colonial Native America.

The impact his writing had on me as a young man may seem hard for people to understand who did not live through the 1960s and early 1970s; these years were a hinge of history when Civil Rights and liberation movements were at high tide. The anti-war struggles against the Vietnam War had reshaped American society. Women's rights and feminism were gaining momentum. The LGBT community was emerging. And in the midst of this era of turmoil and transition, the American Indian Movement (AIM) was making headlines as it demonstrated for Native sovereignty and treaty rights.[4]

AIM was founded in 1968 in Minneapolis, Minnesota. It began as a local community organizing effort among the many urban Native communities in the Twin Cities, but it grew quickly to national prominence. I remember standing out in the snow in those years listening to one of AIM's founders, Dennis Banks, call on all of us who were Native American to unite to reclaim our heritage. In 1971, I supported AIM's "Trail of Broken Treaties" demonstration in Washington, DC; in 1973 I supported the stand-off at Wounded Knee, South Dakota. Both were pivotal confrontations between Native American activists and the Federal government. In 1978

I took part in the "Longest Walk," a demonstration that began on Alcatraz Island in San Francisco, and carried the sacred pipe across the United States to the Washington Monument. I walked on the culmination of this journey with tribal elders; I stood in the July heat with thousands of other Native people when we reached the Capitol to uphold Native sovereignty.

In more ways than one, I had not only talked the talk of Native rights, but quite literally walked the walk. Therefore, the confusion I felt had nothing to do with a lack of political awareness, social consciousness, or historical knowledge. I was not confused about which "side" I was on.[5] I was not uncertain about my own radicalism, or about my solidarity with all those who shared my political convictions as a Native American. I felt "Indian" all the way through on the core concerns of my generation. My problem was strictly spiritual. My fear was that I did not have a firm center in the one place where it counted most: in my religion. In my faith.

As any Native elder will tell you, everything grows from the spirit. The political, social, and economic parts of our lives are inextricably interwoven with our spiritual being. None of my commitments to any of the causes of Native American identity, no matter how sincere, could be genuine if it did not arise from a deep spiritual source. If I was conflicted in my faith as a Native American, I was lost. Unless and until I could resolve my religious identity, the rest would only be shouting into the wind.

So I created a personal ritual. I took what I understood about how to pray in a traditional Native way, adapted that to my circumstances, and began to practice an intimate form of prayer. For more days than I can now remember, I went out at dawn on a rooftop as if it were my own high and lonely place. I drew a circle of cornmeal around me. I stood alone beneath brightening skies or rainy weather, determined to find out if Vine Deloria was right, determined to discover if God was different than what I had been raised to believe.

I did this as a lament, a confession of my own spiritual confusion. I did it because I took my spiritual self seriously. I went seeking some answers to my dilemma, searching for the right path to follow to religious integrity. In short, standing up there on the windswept roof, in the least likely place as the least likely seeker, I began a vision quest.

But was it "a vision quest"? Does what I describe from my own experience qualify as such? How do we define a vision quest? How do we understand it?

In 1890, the same year as the infamous massacre at Wounded Knee (see Chapter Four), James George Frazer published his landmark book, *The Golden Bough.*[6] Frazer, a Scottish anthropologist, pioneered the study of comparative religion and myth as a scientific project. He collated and contrasted religious stories, identifying common themes. In so doing, he set in motion generations of European and American scholarship. He was followed in his research by figures such as Carl Jung, Mircea Eliade, Claude Levi-Strauss, and perhaps most notably, Joseph Campbell, author of *The Hero with a Thousand Faces.*[7]

Among the lines of research all four followed was the question of how human beings search for and obtain spiritual knowledge. These academics sought to trace the origin and nature of the "quest" in human mythology. They studied thousands of stories through scores of cultures. Their conclusions vary, but there is a thread that runs through much of their analysis. A hint of that thread is contained in the title to Campbell's book: the quest made by a heroic figure.

Unpacking the combined academic legacy of anthropologists and psychologists like Jung and Campbell is more than I will attempt to do here, but I will highlight that notion of the quest as being heroic because I believe it opens a door into the difference from the "vision quest" as it is understood by European and Native American cultures.

From the European tradition, we may think of the medieval knight, the Arthurian hero, setting out to seek the Holy Grail. This romantic image speaks to a spiritual psyche of long standing in the West. The story of the valiant spiritual seeker, facing danger and temptation, searching for an elusive prize is a powerful spiritual metaphor for European-based cultures. It is certainly one that is shared by other world communities, but it is a hallmark of Western story-telling.

The Grail legends are classic examples of this understanding. They have long roots in the tribal cultures that created European civilization and their popularity in the many variations on the King Arthur saga indicate how strongly the myth of the hero is present in this shared history. I also suggest that they blend into European interpretations of Christianity. The "hero" narrative associated with a "quest" borrows from the Bible. Galahad and Jesus have similar attributes and associations.

The hero must be pure in heart. The hero must face temptations. The hero must discover what no one else can find. In the religious context of the Europeans, the quest becomes more and more the territory of the special person. Not just anyone can decide to go looking for the Holy Grail. Not just anyone can perform a true vision quest. Only people like Jesus or Galahad may be "good enough" to take this epic journey.

I highlight this tendency in Western spirituality not as a definitive statement about the European experience in myth, but as a point of comparison to Native American concepts of a "quest." Like Europeans, Native communities could interpret the quest as a specialized endeavor. Some nations understood it as a shamanic quest, although not with the same emphasis on the nobility of such a person. However, far more Native nations understood the quest to be something almost every person could pursue.

This is significant because it changes the way we think about a "quest." To capture the Native American understanding of a vision quest, it is necessary to let go of some of the European interpretations attached to that term. Even more importantly, unless we can separate Galahad and Jesus in our minds, we may miss the Native perspective on who Jesus was, what he experienced, and what he taught as a Native messiah.

To understand the Native American concept of a sacred quest, we can pick up where the Western scholars have left off: from Gilgamesh to Frodo, the quest is the process, defined by every culture, by which human beings search for the holy. The object of that search may be God, or wisdom, or a Holy Grail. Each religious tradition sets the destination for those who believe, and each tradition creates a roadmap for how to get there. Some quests require physical endurance, some require mental concentration. Some can last for days, some for a lifetime. The definitions are as varied as the destinations.

As the ancient idea of the quest spread around the world different communities developed their own understanding of not only how the quest should be undertaken, but who could attempt it. In some cultures the quest increasingly became the realm of religious specialists and the type of person who practiced the vision quest narrowed: shamans, mystics, saints, knights of valor. In Native America, however, the door remained much more open. Prior to 1492, the vision quest was a threshold accessible to millions of Native people.

While there are variations on the theme of a quest in the many different traditions of Native America, there are some basic elements that are constant and appear over and over again.

First, there is a time of preparation. The quest is intentional. It is a planned movement toward the sacred. Therefore, the person must be ready for this journey. There is always a spiritual prelude to the quest, a time of prayer and purification. These acts cleanse the person both physically and mentally, making him or her ready to come into the presence of the holy in a respectful way.

Among the most common practices of preparation is the sweat lodge. The sweat lodge is a form of communal worship and prayer. It takes place in a small structure (the lodge) usually made from bent saplings tied together into a dome-like shape. They were covered with animal hides in the past and, more commonly now, in canvas. Within this lodge a small circle is shaped in the earth at the center of the structure where hot stones are placed from a fire outside the lodge which is tended by a ceremonial helper.

Once the participants in the service have entered the lodge by a single opening, that opening is covered and water is poured over the stones. In the womb-like environment, the person designated to lead the service begins a series of chants and prayers that are joined by all of those in the lodge. The experience is intimate and intense. The men or women in the sweat lodge (traditionally participating in their own separate lodges) are naked in the darkness, aware of being with others, but also confined by the darkness into their own physicality. The cleansing of the sweat lodge is not only the release of toxins from the body, but a deep focus on healing prayer. When people complete a sweat lodge cycle of prayer, they traditionally bathe in clean water, emerging refreshed as if they were newborn into a spiritual world. The sweat lodge is an integral part of preparation for the Native American quest. Other disciplines are used as well such as periods of fasting, celibacy, and meditation. Together these intentional practices underscore the importance of preparation for a Native quest.

The second element common to any Native American quest is the presence of others. Any man or woman setting out on a quest in the Native American tradition would have at least one other person and often a circle of family and friends helping them. They would be under the care of an elder, usually a respected "medicine" man or woman, i.e., a recognized spiritual teacher of the people. These supporters would join in the rituals of purification. They would be a base of prayer to sustain the good intentions of the quester. One or more would even accompany the person to the site chosen for the quest and remain nearby to help through ongoing prayers and songs.

This kind of help is important because the third element of a Native American quest is the nature of it as a challenge. The quest is not an easy experience to undergo. It is not unknown for a traditional Native vision quest to last up to four days without food or water. During that time the person stays awake, remaining in one sacred space, usually a lonely place in the natural world where he or she is exposed to the elements. The vision quest is not for the faint of heart and it is not something to be taken lightly. There is a physical dimension to it, a test of a person's endurance and resolve. Preparation and support are crucial because the quest is demanding. Over time, other cultures lost the expectation that members of the faith community would be willing to undergo a physical challenge to embody their faith. The Native American tradition retains this value in its understanding of the vision quest.

The fourth aspect of the Native quest is difficult to translate from the original, but perhaps the best term for it would be the nature of the quest as a lament. In some Native languages, the quest is described as a time of "crying." Psychology and theology within Native American culture merge in the relationship between human beings and God. The quest begins in a recognition that human beings are in need of help. The birth-like experience of the sweat lodge is mirrored in the quest where a helpless person cries out to the Parent-God for support and understanding. The quest is nurture. It is humility. It is not a test of how strong and brave a person can be, but rather, how vulnerable she or he can be.

These four basic components describe the classic Native American vision quest: preparation, community, challenge, and lament. While the idea of a quest, a search for deeper meaning, was part of the spiritual heritage of almost every human society through history, it took this basic form in pre-Columbian North America.

It was a process that most, if not all, young people were expected to undertake. It was an experience that a person could repeat more than once in life. It was a quest that was visionary, but it was also something more. The Native American quest was pragmatic, designed to produce transformation. It was not a private esoteric experience, but a way in which the community prepared, supported and developed functioning members of society. The quest was a tool, a method for seeding back into the community persons who understood both the spiritual nature of life and their role in it.

This is why traditional Native people would often receive a name change after returning from a vision quest. They would go out into the wilderness to encounter God with one name, but they would return with another. The name change implied the transformation. It announced that the person had become someone new, someone with a renewed skill and purpose in life. The community would acknowledge and adopt the name as a sign of spiritual transformation, drawing in both the individual and his or her vision into the daily life of the nation.

So, did I deserve a name change after my experience on the roof all those years ago? Had I undertaken the quest as my ancestors understood it? Was I transformed?

Yes and no.

No, my rooftop experience was not a classic vision quest by traditional Native American standards. I did not have the benefit of purification rituals, community support, or a ceremony of return. My name stayed the same.

Yes, it was a quest in the spirit of the quest as my culture understands it. My reading of Vine Deloria's book was a time of preparation. It cleansed me of many of my old assumptions. It forced me into a new place of awareness. It set me on my course to confront myself and to learn more about the God I said I wanted to serve.

Yes, it was a challenge in a lonely place, not just physically, but emotionally. Standing on that roof I felt exposed to more than weather. I felt the loneliness of confusion. Doubt is an isolating feeling, it forces a person into a narrow space, a hidden space, and denies the easy comforts of trust that cushion us in our religious pieties. When we are unsure about what we believe, we truly stand naked before God, stripped of those dogmas that we wear like denominational clothing to give us a sense of security. So, yes, it was hard to be alone on the roof. It was hard to face the possibility I was a betrayer of my own people, a sell-out to a foreign ideology, a false prophet of a false god.

Finally, yes, it was a quest my ancestors would have understood because I believe it was a time of transformation. I did discover something up on the roof. I was not alone. I did receive a vision. And I was changed. My name may have been the same, but the person using it was not. In the next chapter I will tell you about my vision, but for now I want to stay focused on the process by which I received it. I do so to honor the Native tradition of the quest before I talk about the vision.

I believe we live in an age when the idea of a quest has been cheapened. This is a time when "spirituality" has been so commercialized it

has become a commodity. Native American traditions have been strip-
mined to supply the window dressing for pseudo-religious practices.
Self-proclaimed "shamans" abound. Self-styled "medicine men" and
"medicine women" are abundant. They offer sweat lodges and vision
quests for people to experience for a price. They promise to give their
disciples "power animals" and "spirit guides." They use drumming as
a hypnotic tool to make their hybrid rituals seem authentic.

When I walked out onto the roof alone, I was only a young
man looking for meaning. I was not attempting to design some fast
track system of spirituality for others to follow. I was not imagining
that what I was doing was a genuine esoteric practice from Native
American tradition. I would not, could not, buy, package or sell what
I experienced. My quest was my quest, not a formula for anyone else
to follow. It was a step out into the unknown, a longing of the heart,
a willingness to risk being foolish for the sake of an encounter that
cannot be explained, much less sold.

I do not want to hurry on to the subject of spiritual vision because
I believe people in our postmodern culture are in far too much of
a hurry as it is. We want instant spirituality, instant visions, instant
meaning. The vision quest is not a form of Google. It is not a formula that can be bought. It is not a kind of magic into which a
person can be instructed or inducted. Rather, from the traditional
view of Native America, it is a gradual, difficult, intentional effort to
engage what we cannot buy or sell, define or control: mystery. The
mystery of who we are, why we are, and what we are to become.

Without mystery there is no quest. That is the first principle and
the second is like unto it: the purpose of the quest itself is not to
solve the mystery, but to deepen it. In the current rush to enlightenment, many people of this age assume they can use Native American
tradition as a shortcut to the answers that elude them. They invest in
the vision quest as magic because they believe it will reveal something
hidden to them, give them the secret knowledge they desire, offer
them a sense of control over their lives as spiritual beings.

In fact, the purpose of the vision quest is to do none of these
things. The focus of the quest is mystery; the process of the quest is

mystery; the outcome of the quest is mystery. The reason is simple: since the purpose of the quest is to encounter God, the source of the mystery, the nature of the quest must be in mystery from start to finish. In essence, because the quest is the human search for God, there is no point at which the human ceases to function as human, or at which God ceases to be God. Therefore, the limited, finite nature of the human being undertaking the quest is always just that: limited and finite. We are beings conditioned by mystery, defined by mystery, because we can never truly know the full mind of God. We cannot work our magic to steal a bit of the power of God or the wisdom of God.

Not that we have not tried over the centuries. Many spiritual traditions throughout history that we call "mystery religions" promised human beings a chance to escape their reality and magically become inducted into the secret knowledge of the immortal gods. Ironically, the goal of these mystery cults was to do away with mystery. And it was not only a few unusual spiritual communities that have tried to evade mystery; I believe there is a thread of that desire that runs through most human religions. The shaman consuming an hallucinogen to fly to an alternate reality believes that he or she can transcend the bonds of human reality; but, to be fair, so do many of us who invest ourselves in a particular religious truth claim. There is at least some notion of overcoming mystery implicit in our faith. Whether we follow Jesus or Muhammad or the Buddha, we believe we have found the answer, the path that leads out of the finite terrain of our everyday existence. Like the shaman, we seek transcendence, that mystical step over the threshold of the finite into the hidden dimension of the infinite. We may not think that this transition will occur instantly, we may not imagine that we can control its happening in any way at all, but we still place some part of our faith in the hope of knowing. We believe we have found in this dimension a hint of the dimension to come. Not only will what we believe permit us a small taste of the next reality, eventually it may allow us to pass beyond the mystery to see the truth face to face.

And yet, while we may have a deep longing to finally know and understand what we hold sacred, the vision quest has nothing to do with fulfilling that longing because it has nothing to do with transcendence. Despite what Arthurian legend may have suggested, despite what mystery cults may have promised, and even despite our own personal level of longing to peek behind the curtain of meaning, the quest is not an answer. It is a deeper question.

I realize that my opinion about the nature and role of the vision quest is a little counter-intuitive for many people, including many Native Americans. After all, if the quest is not going to give us some answers, then what good is it? That's a fair question. My reply is that the quest is not about transcendence, but transformation. And transformation is not necessarily transcendence. In fact, it can be just the opposite. Transformation can mean a grounding into reality, a deepening into the finite. Transformation is a process of forming a human life from the substance of that life itself. Seen in this context, the quest is not an escape from reality, but a passage into an even deeper reality. It is not designed to reveal something hidden, but to alert us to something in plain sight. It does not give us a secret wisdom, but makes us reconsider what we have always known. The quest is an invitation to go deeper.

When I first went out on my rooftop I was looking for answers. I wanted the bigger picture of my life, some experience that would show me what I thought I could not see. I hoped that I could transcend my limited reality and be shown the path to follow to make me the disciple I wanted to be. My intention in this way was not very different from countless other human beings who have sought a transcendent moment. Such moments are possible. Transcendence can occur. People can have the scales fall from their eyes, be swept up in a rapture divine, be given a glimpse of eternity. The only problem is: we have no formula for making that happen. Transcendent experience, from my perspective, is wholly at the initiative of God. It is not something we can obtain through our own diligence or by virtue of our own deserving.

The quest is not a tool of transcendence. It is a method of transformation. It begins very much with our own initiative. It truly is a case of our going out to find God, not God coming to find us. It is humble in expectation, an experience truly bounded by our finite nature and located in our earthy reality, which is why it is our lament. Looking back, my choice of an urban rooftop for my first quest was more than appropriate because fewer places could be more mundane. I did not go up to Sinai to find my God. I went up to the roof of my house.

The transformation of the quest begins in this celebration of the human. The fact that a fragile, finite creature would take the initiative to "find" God is the first stage of the quest's transformative experience. It is the hinge point, the turning toward transformation. The quest begins with the mystery of our own self-awareness: we understand that we are fragile and limited creatures, and we also understand that there is something greater than ourselves. The spiritual audacity of a quest is that we want to connect the two. We are aware of our reality and the reality of the sacred; where the two come into contact is the location of the quest. Whether we physically choose to carry out our quest on a mountain top or a rooftop makes no difference. The real location is the nexus point of spiritual awareness. We do not leave the finite. We do not enter the infinite. We stand at the place of intersection. We do not transcend our own reality, much less the reality of the infinite, but we are positioned for transformation because when the mundane becomes a vehicle for the sacred, things change.

The quest is sacramental. It is the process by which the substance of our everyday reality becomes transformed. How this happens is a mystery. Why it happens is a mystery. But in effect, we take the initiative to place ourselves at this hinge point because we believe that something wonderful happens when the two are brought together. When I had my experience on the roof I did not outwardly appear any different, but by an inward working of grace, by a touch of the mystery of God, I was changed. My substance shifted. My spiritual location shifted, even if only by inches, pointing me to a new trajectory toward the sacred.

The quest, therefore, is the reverse of intentionally placing ourselves in harm's way. It is an act of placing ourselves in grace's way.

We are looking for that point of intersection where we think we are most likely to encounter God. These locations, which we sometimes call the thin places of our reality, are not defined by geography, but by intention. While I understand that there are many geographical locations that people revere, I do not believe that any of these places are magical portals to transformation. The key to the seeker's quest is not in finding just the right piece of holy real estate on which to stand, but rather in so preparing his or her awareness that any space he or she occupies can become thin through faith.

The quest is the sacrament of the seeker. It is the embodiment of, the celebration of, the ordinary in communion with the truly transcendent, the presence of the God who cannot be fully known much less manipulated. It is the numinous point of contact where transformation can occur because the initiative of the finite person meets the initiative of the infinite Person. The quest is the action of the seeker to move into this spiritual space. The shift to the location where the mind can be receptive to an encounter with God begins in the inner reality of the seeker. It begins in the interior landscape of perception, awareness, and consciousness. There is a mindset to the quest, an awareness that must be in place no matter what the physical location of the seeker may be.

Long ago The Buddha helped us to understand this aspect of the quest. He told us that no matter where we were in time and space, we could sit down, be quiet, and open our minds to a transformative level of awareness. The meditation that he taught is this internal form of the quest. In the same way Native American tradition says that we must purify our awareness if we are going out to seek the holy. The cleansing act of letting go of daily chatter, of distractions and desires, takes place in Zen meditation as surely as it does in the Native American sweat lodge. The first step of the quest begins inside. It begins in preparation. It is the seeker's intentional effort to enter into the real so deeply that he or she comes out on the other side.

The physical setting of the quest can be helpful to the seeker because it is conducive to this level of calm concentration, but there is no magic door through which he or she passes into transcendence.

There is only the mystery of communion, of that sacramental chemistry by which the mundane is transformed into the holy. It can happen with bread and wine. It can also happen with breath and blood, within the finite reality of the human body. When we place ourselves in the path of grace, when we open our minds and hearts to receive the presence of God, we are in the thin place of transformation. The quest becomes tangible because it becomes embodied. It is not a flight of the mind to imagine transcendence, but a movement of the very substance of human life to the place of meeting we can only describe as incarnation.

The Incarnation is God's vision quest.

That sentence is the most concise way to express the doctrine of the Incarnation from the Native American viewpoint. The Incarnation has all of the classic elements of a quest. God experiences a time of preparation (the first vision quest of Jesus). God expresses a need for the support of community (the second vision quest of Jesus). God endures a test on behalf of all people (the third vision quest of Jesus). God makes a transforming lament that heals the world (the fourth vision quest of Jesus). From the perspective of Native American tradition, the idea that God would take human form to experience the vision quest makes sense. Jesus becomes one of the human family, the tribe of the human beings, in order to do the work of transformation that a quest is designed to do. For Native people, contact with God does not occur only in the abstractions of the mind, but in the everyday physical engagement of the body. The sweat lodge is physical. The vision quest is physical. The experience of God is physical. The Incarnation, therefore, is transformation made tangible.

The human quest is the risk of intimacy with God. It is going out to attempt to discover God and enter into communion with God. But without the Incarnation, that level of communion would remain as disembodied as relationships on the Internet. A message might be passed between us, a kind of cosmic photo of God shared on the digital screen of spirituality, but the flesh and blood intimacy of physical contact would elude us. God would remain a dream, not an experience. The graphic story of the gospels tells us how God lived through the quest. It allows us to enter into God's own time of preparation. It lets us become among those friends who support God in this intention. It shows us how God does go out into "thin" places to seek a deeper reality. It describes what God sees and hears during the quest. It explains the nature of the sacrifice involved and it reveals the final outcome of the quest as the finite and the infinite merge into a vision beyond anything we might have imagined.

The New Testament is a vision quest story, an invitation to us to step into the vision quest of God. This quest is transformative. It is not the transcendent myth of a shaman far removed from human experience, doing things we could never hope to do, flying away from us into an ethereal realm reserved only for the few; instead, it is the earth-bound story of a flesh and blood seeker who lives in the midst of the mundane, using what is at hand to turn the common into the extraordinary. The quest is not an escape, but a rooting into reality: a celebration of the everyday, the physical, the sensual, and the experiential.

Because of God's vision quest, our quests can take on a deeper dimension. We can follow the story of the incarnate seeker to focus our own search into an interior geography of faith that can bring us closer to our goal, intimacy with God. No matter where we are, we can step into the space once occupied by Jesus and find a real presence there to speak to us. God's quest can transform us, not by lifting us out of ourselves but by grounding us into the joy and struggle of being human. Therefore, walking the way of Christ is walking the stations of the quest as much as those of the cross. We follow Jesus into the place of transformation.

As a young man I tried to find faith in the midst of doubt. I instinctively sought some way to transform my reality from a painful experience into a healing vision. I turned to the wisdom of my own ancestors to perform a quest in the spirit of Native American tradition. I tried to create a sacred space with the most mundane things I had at hand: a rooftop and a box of cornmeal. I did not know if my quest would take me away from my faith in Jesus. I did not know if I would discover myself to be a hypocrite, but I decided to take that risk. I walked out to a lonely place to find intimacy with God. I experienced transformation by meeting transcendence. I joined the story of incarnation.

What follows in this book is a description of vision, the mystery at the heart of the quest, and of the visions of God as I have come to understand them as a Native American theologian. In sharing my thoughts I have no sense of having an experience that is rare or unique. As a Native person, I believe we are all called to make our own vision quests. We are called by our doubts or our hope. We are called by ancient myths or new mysteries. In answering that call, we each make our vision quest in our own way. We have our own traditions. And yet, we walk a similar path:

1. We prepare ourselves to answer the call to a quest.
2. We seek the support of friends and mentors.
3. We accept the discipline of our intentions.
4. We express our deepest longings.

These four sacred directions of the vision quest are the guidelines used by Native American people for centuries. They are so simple because they are so common. They are accessible to every person. We may be inspired by the romantic stories of the heroes of our traditions, but we are as called as they were to make our vision quest. Jesus is not Galahad. He was a person, a human being, just like you and me when he felt the call to make a quest. Four times he went out seeking the vision of God. Four times he followed the four simple steps of the Native American tradition. We can follow him. We can read the descriptions of his experience, see the visions through his eyes, and learn from him about intimacy with God. His quest and ours can be the same.

Chapter 2

THE VISION

The twentieth century has produced a world of conflicting visions, intense emotions, and unpredictable events, and the opportunities for grasping the substance of life have faded as the pace of activity has increased. Electronic media shuffle us through a myriad of experiences which would have baffled earlier generations and seem to produce in us a strange isolation from the reality of human history. Our heroes fade into mere personality, are consumed and forgotten, and we avidly seek more avenues to express our humanity. Reflection is the most difficult of all our activities because we are no longer able to establish relative priorities from the multitude of sensations that engulf us. Times such as these seem to illuminate the classic expressions of eternal truths and great wisdom comes to stand out in the crowd of ordinary maxims.

Vine Deloria, Jr.

From his "Forward" to *Black Elk Speaks,* 1979[1]

"A world of conflicting visions," that is how Vine Deloria described our religious and social reality when he wrote his introduction to one of the most influential books on Native American spirituality ever published. *Black Elk Speaks* first appeared in 1932. It was presented by John G. Neihardt, a poet and writer, as his interview with a traditional Lakota medicine man, Black Elk. It contains the extended vision Black Elk experienced as a young boy as well as the story of his later life. It is a glimpse, therefore, into a lost world because Black Elk was in the last generation of Plains Indian people to live in freedom on their own land. Black Elk was a relative of Crazy Horse and a contemporary of

George Armstrong Custer. He remembered the coming of the white man to the Dakotas, the building of the railroads, the death of the buffalo, the wars fought between Lakota warriors and the cavalry, including the historic battle of the Little Big Horn. His memories are history. They are tradition. Black Elk captured the imagination of readers because he recounted a time and place that had ceased to exist, a nostalgic and haunting story of the pride and wisdom of Native America before the conquest by Europeans.

Black Elk Speaks remains in print today, but its high tide of popularity began in the late 1960s and early 1970s when it was discovered by both Native American and non-Native audiences as an authentic voice of the religious tradition of America's indigenous people. It is not an exaggeration to say it influenced how we think about Native American tradition, even though, as Vine says in his preface, "debates center on the question of Neihardt's literary intrusions into Black Elk's system of beliefs and some scholars have said that the book reflects more of Neihardt than it does of Black Elk."[2]

Parsing out which words were Black Elk's and which were Neihardt's is a scholarly exercise I will leave to other writers. My purpose here is to invite us into the realm of vision, and few paths into this subject are as engaging as *Black Elk Speaks.* Whether it is the unadulterated narrative of a medicine man or the glossed memories of a romantic poet, it is still the cultural place marker for what we consider to be a Native American "vision quest."

If you have not read *Black Elk Speaks* the centrality of its impact on our understanding of "vision" from the Native American theological point of view may not make sense, so please let me take a moment to offer a sketch of what Black Elk saw. It will be only a fragment of the complete visionary picture, but hopefully it will be enough to illustrate how Black Elk's narrative influenced (and continues to influence) how we conceive of a spiritual "vision."

In his chapter called "The Great Vision," Neihardt records the words of Black Elk describing his falling ill at nine years of age. He lost mobility and his body seemed to swell. He lay in his teepee, watched over by his parents. Suddenly he saw two men "coming from the clouds."[3] They told him to accompany them. Black Elk's physical symptoms disappeared and, as he walked outside his teepee, he was caught up by a cloud and taken into another world:

> *Then there was nothing but the air and the swiftness of the little cloud that bore me and those two men still leading me up to where white clouds were piled like mountains on a wide blue plain, and in them thunder beings lived and leaped and flashed.*[4]

The vision continues as a mystical creature, a bay horse, narrates to Black Elk what is being revealed to him. More horses appear, "their manes were lightning and there was thunder in their nostrils,"[5] from each of the points of the compass, "and there were horses, horses everywhere—a whole sky full of horses dancing around me."[6] These herds of horses play a central role in his vision. They embody the spiritual powers traditional Native Americans associate with the cardinal directions. Black Elk observes these spirit animals as they escort him into deeper levels of his vision.

The vision shifts and Black Elk is brought to a great rainbow teepee where six old men are sitting, "and they looked older than men can ever be—old like hills, like stars."[7] These ancient beings present a cup of water to Black Elk, "the power to make live,"[8] and a bow, "the power to destroy."[9] The elders, Grandfather figures, rise up to enormous size and prophesy to Black Elk ultimately showing him the tree of life that will shelter and prosper his people. But this bright vision is challenged by another reality as Black Elk is shown a time when the earth will be "silent in a sick green light"[10] and "the hills look up afraid" and everywhere "the cries of frightened birds and sounds of fleeing wings"[11] – the vision of the attack on his people by the blue coated Europeans. It is a dark and ominous portent, but in the end it is redeemed by a promise of healing,

> *Then when the many little voices ceased, the great Voice said: "Behold the circle of the nation's hoop, for it is holy,*

being endless, and thus all powers shall be one power in the people without end. Now they shall break camp and go forth upon the red road, and your Grandfathers shall walk with them.[12]

These Grandfathers instruct Black Elk into the mysteries of his life, including his role as a healer. The Grandfather, "he of where the sun shines continually,"[13] gives Black Elk a sacred pipe and tells him "With this pipe you shall walk the earth, and whatever sickens there you shall make well."[14] Finally, the sixth Grandfather, "he who was the Spirit of the Earth,"[15] appears to Black Elk with "hair long and white, his face was all in wrinkles and his eyes were deep and dim," and slowly transforms before him into a young boy, which Black Elk recognizes: ". . . I knew that he was myself with all the years that would be mine at last."[16] This spirit tells Black Elk he is receiving his vision because his people will have great need of him in the days to come.

Many other visions are part of his Great Vision: images of eagles and buffalo, of young men and maidens, of a sacred nation walking the sacred way. To fully appreciate the complexity and intricacy of the total vision one would need to read the book, but let us bring it to a close here by saying that at the end of his experience Black Elk is led by the original two angelic figures back to his home camp, where he is still lying sick as a boy: "I could see my people's village far ahead of me, and I walked very fast, for I was homesick now. Then I saw my mother and my father bending over a sick boy that was myself. And as I entered the teepee, someone was saying: 'The boy is coming to; you had better give him some water.'"[17]

To what can we compare an epic vision such as Black Elk's? The Book of Daniel? The Book of Revelation? Yes, exactly. Black Elk is the Native American equivalent of the prophet Daniel or John of Patmos. The visions he recounts are poetic images that are visual prophecy. They are spiritual ciphers for deeper theological meaning, a grand narrative of cosmic forces, all revolving around the central theme of revelation. There are animal figures, angelic beings, a host of elders, a mixture of colors, and mystic words of what is to come, all connected to this single person who, like Daniel and John, offers his testimony to us as an invitation into mystery.

Christians from the Western tradition can look back to the visionaries of the Hebrew scriptures; Christians from the Native American tradition can do the same with Black Elk. His narrative, like Daniel's and John's, inspires a range of reactions. We can interpret these visions as imaginative poetry, spiritual prophecy, or private delusions. Whether or not we accept them, they are the provocative catalysts for some of our deepest theological questions: Do people really have visions like these? Are they real? Are they messages from God or just day dreams of an overly fervent faith? What do they mean, not only literally, but as mysterious elements in our religious tradition? Should we treat them as genuine encounters with the divine or as "religious CGI," special effects that are stunning but fake?

In his own prophetic way, Vine Deloria said that Black Elk's meaning would come to us more clearly in an age when our heroes were only celebrities and our truths only choices from a menu of maxims. Maybe he was right. Ours is an age when vision has become more the property of Hollywood than of prophecy. Many people, Christians included, skip over the Book of Revelation as being either too convoluted to be of value or as the haunt of biblical fanatics who want to push an apocalyptic agenda. In the same way, Native American medicine men can be appreciated as colorful characters from America's exotic past or as "witch doctors" who made up stories to impress the gullible.

Our starting point to understand vision, from both the Native American and Christian perspective, must begin in this cultural climate that Vine anticipated when the level of our technology has rendered the idea of authentic spiritual vision suspect by making it too familiar. We trust the media, not the message. After all, Disney can produce dancing horses for us in any color we want.

The path into vision that I want to chart is the broad area between the extremes of skepticism and literalism. Unlike religious ideologies that have staked out the Book of Revelation for strip-mining apocalyptic fantasies to sell to an anxious but lucrative audience, or contemporary gnostic spiritualities that have mined sources like Black Elk to merchandise "spirit helpers" and "dream catchers," I want to de-commercialize vision.

The middle ground of vision is hard to find between these extremes of doubt and exploitation, but it is there beneath the inflated expectations both extremes have created. It is not better special effects or quicker enlightenment, but the quiet experience of the man or woman who follows the call of vision as a quest. In this sense, vision is not a shout, but a whisper; not an extravaganza of images, but a single picture.

When I went out on the rooftop over forty years ago I had a vision. It was not a vision like Black Elk, or Daniel, or John of Patmos, but it was a vision. It did not include a cast of characters numbering in the hundreds, but only a single character. It did not announce a grand design for the rest of my life, but only suggested a word of meaning that I could carry with me.

I value this vision and share it because I want to rescue vision for all of us who live in an age that has few heroes and many cheap options for revelation. I believe that many of us have been shy about speaking of our own visions. We know they cannot duplicate the wonders of Black Elk. We also hesitate because vision has been so expropriated by fringe elements of religion we do not want to face ridicule. Therefore, we remain quiet about what we have seen.

If I break this silence and speak of one of the visions I have had, do I run a risk? Yes, I am certain I do, especially in a time when spiritual vision is so suspect. But I believe the risk is worth it because, if we do not reclaim the presence of vision in our lives, we abandon the field to those who would occupy it for their own ends. In sharing my vision, I claim it is neither a rarity nor a commodity. In fact, it is a quite common, simple fact of our spiritual lives, an option available to any person who seeks it through his or her own quest.

As I said in the last chapter, the quest in Native American theology is not reserved for the specialist. Black Elk was not the only Native person to have a vision. There were thousands, even millions who did. Over the centuries, as the vision quest was practiced in a great many traditional Native communities, generations of Native men and women went out in order to go within: that is, they made an intentional effort to receive a vision from God.

We know very few of these visions. Perhaps some were as grand as the one Black Elk experienced. Certainly there were powerful visions that were such intense catalysts they propelled ordinary people into extraordinary spiritual teachers. Among these great Native prophets were people such as Hiawatha and Dekanawida of the Haudenosaunee (Iroquois), Handsome Lake of the Seneca, and Tenskwatawa of the Shawnee.[18] Like the prophets of ancient Israel, these were people whose visions were so profound they became forces for religious renewal and political change. Dekanawida brought the Great Law of Peace to the six nations of the Iroquois Confederacy, uniting them into a nation just as the twelve tribes of Israel became a nation by adopting the statutes God gave to Moses.[19] Tenskwatawa inspired Tecumseh to lead armed resistance against the European occupiers of Native lands just as Samuel inspired David to take up the fight for Israel.

Great deeds come from great visions, and history records how this process has happened in global cultures throughout the world. Understandably, these kinds of dramatic visions are few and far between. They are not the norm, but the exception. This does not mean, however, that only a handful of chosen prophets are privileged to receive a vision. In the Christian tradition we know of a great many other mystics and saints whose visions were recorded. In both the Eastern and Western Church there are long lists of these men and women, and their visions continue to be recounted, studied, and interpreted. They are a bibliography of vision for Christian theology.

In the same way, there are scores of Native Americans who have had holy visions that inspired their community. Some of these people we know; some we do not. And there are many more whose visions brought meaning into their own lives, even if they went unrecognized by anyone else. We know this because we know that the practice of the vision quest was widespread and generic. Unlike our hesitant age when we doubt our own ability to receive a vision, and doubt even more the claim of others to have had one, traditional Native American society was a culture that not only affirmed the vision quest experience, but encouraged it. The path toward vision, therefore, the middle way we wish to discover, is a broad avenue running through Native American spiritual history. It is not the narrow way of the apocalyptic preacher or the New Age shaman, but the open road that many, if not all, people can choose to follow.

It is the road I chose when I stepped out onto the roof. More by instinct than training, I believed God was accessible to me if I would only do what my ancestors had done: make the vision quest. Ironically, in doing so, I was following in the footsteps of Black Elk. Although his first great vision came to him during an illness as a child, in later life he made his traditional vision quest. In *Black Elk Speaks* he describes his vision quest experience (which translates as "going out lamenting") in detail. It contains all of the classic elements of a quest:

> *After the long winter of waiting, it was my first duty to go out lamenting. So after the first rain storm I began to get ready. When going out to lament it is necessary to choose a wise old medicine man, who is quiet and generous, to help. There was a good and wise old medicine man by the name of Few Tails, who was glad to help me. First he told me to fast for four days, and I could have only water during that time. Then, after he had offered the pipe, I had to purify myself in a sweat lodge, which we made with willow boughs set in the ground and bent down to make a round top. Over this we tied a bison robe. In the middle we put hot stones, and when I was in there, Few Tails poured water on the stones. I sang to the spirits while I was in there being purified. Then the old man rubbed me all over with sage. He then braided my hair, and I was naked except that I had a bison robe to wrap around me while lamenting in the night, for although the days were warm, the nights were cold. All I carried was*

*the sacred pipe. . . . It is necessary to go far away from people
to lament, so Few Tails and I started from Pine Ridge. We
came to a high hill close to Grass Creek. There was nobody
there but the old man and myself and the sky and the earth.
But the place was full of people; for the spirits were there.*[20]

In this way, Black Elk undertook the vision quest, the lament that
generations of Native people have done for centuries: "Standing in
the center of the sacred place . . . I began to cry, and while crying
I had to say: O Great Spirit, accept my offerings! O make me
understand!"[21]

In 1973, standing in the center of my cornmeal circle, high on
a rooftop as far away from people as I could get, I had to cry out
exactly the same thing. I wanted God, the Great Spirit, to help me
understand. And God did help me. I did receive a vision. In my own
way, I stepped into the circle with my ancestors. I shared in their
experience.

What Black Elk records he saw on the high hill close to Grass
Creek was a series of visions befitting a great medicine man. He saw
the tree of life, the hoop of the nation, the spirit of Crazy Horse.
But among these great visions was a single moment that has unique
meaning for me. At one point in his quest, Black Elk says that he
noticed a small bird, "a black swallow flying all around me, singing,
and stopped upon a bush not far away."[22] That image has power for
me because what I saw one cold morning on a high building close
to Harvard University was something very similar. I saw a black bird.
I saw a crow.

Let me stop for a moment before I say more because at times like
this, when I share the substance of my first vision, I have to smile
because I think I almost hear the "so that's it?" reaction from my listeners, or in this case, my readers. I can almost hear the words inside
their heads: You saw a crow? A bird? One bird? And that's all? That's
the vision?

Yes, that's it. Not quite as impressive as the Book of Revelation
or *Black Elk Speaks*. Not a burning bush or a rainbow teepee. Just a

bird. A single bird. Like Black Elk, I saw a black bird, but in my case, it was a very large, very black, crow.

As usual that morning I had been doing my lament, my praying for God to give me understanding. I stood in the center of my circle and turned to each of the six directions, drawing a spiritual gyroscope around myself to keep me in balance as I imagined myself stepping out into the mystery of God. I had been praying for quite a while, looking out, but with my eyes closed so I could remain within, when, quite unexpectedly, I felt someone watching me.

This feeling is one I believe most people have experienced, but find difficult to define. It is that odd sensation that overtakes us when, for no reason we can clearly articulate, we believe we are being observed, watched. When that happens, we usually look around, which is exactly what I did on that gray Massachusetts morning. I looked around. And there, only a couple of yards away, sat an enormous black crow perched on the low wall that ran around the rooftop, staring directly at me with the obsidian eyes so characteristic of its species.

It did not move. I did not move. I stared back, almost holding my breath, without any idea of what I should be doing except to remain quiet and pay attention. In that time, that strange vision quest time, all of the ordinary sounds around me (the distant traffic of a waking city) suddenly ceased. Nothing moved. Nothing made a noise. The crow and I were together in a soundless space. We were nowhere. We were everywhere. The time was now. The time was later. It felt alien. It felt intimate. I was me. I was not me. The only way to describe the encounter is to use this kind of paradoxical, poetic language.

The vision was much more than what I physically saw. That's why it strikes me as funny because on the surface all I saw was a crow sitting on a rooftop with me. But when that simple encounter is placed into the context of a vision quest, into the intentional intersection between the sacred and the finite, it begins to look, and sound, and feel much different.

There is no rational explanation. My vision of the crow is as beyond logic as Black Elk's sky full of dancing ponies. I cannot prove the truth of what I say any more than he could, any more than any

Christian mystic or Native American medicine man. I can only tell my story and, by so doing, invite my listeners to step over into an alternate reality, a place of mystery that the human quest for divine understanding must always inhabit.

As the crow and I remained fixed in one another's gaze, and as the stillness around us blocked out any extraneous sound, I heard a holy voice. It was holy to me because it was exactly where I was: both within and without at the same time. It was a voice that I could hear in my mind, but that I did not generate. It was not me speaking. In the same way, I believe it was not the crow speaking, even though it was coming from the crow. I used to laugh when I would recount this part of my vision to seminary students in my classes on Native American theology. I would tell them, "No, the crow's beak did not move as she spoke to me, but yes, she was speaking to me." The crow was the bearer of a message, the channel through which the voice flowed, the focal point for the sacred and the mundane to connect.

Visions are messages. They are messages transmitted through the medium of our senses. We see things, hear things, even feel or smell things that we accept as real. But these images and sensations are not bound by our senses. They exist just beyond our grasp. We do not generate or control them. We cannot fix them into a particular time or space. Instead, we occupy a spiritual proximity to the source of our vision, a tangent point between the infinite and the finite. We never completely know how things happen or for how long they happen. We only know that they did happen and that they have left us with some meaning we need to understand.

In my case, my senses told me that a strange black bird and I were in the presence of a mystical voice, a word that was being spoken to us, through us, around us, and beyond us. It was as if my prayers to the six directions, my gyroscope of spiritual balance, had momentarily been sent spinning. When the sacred finally did arrive to answer my quest, it knocked all of my sense of control out of equilibrium. I was no longer standing on a roof. I was no longer standing beneath a sky. I was not in any place other than a sacred space, a holy ground, and the voice of something far greater than my reality was sending me a message: *Do not be afraid. There are two paths to follow, but one path to find. Be patient.* This was the message the crow brought to me. In that timeless instant of contact with its spirit, these were the words I heard. I might say more accurately, these were the words that wrapped themselves around me. I stood in the midst of them. I was surrounded by them, upheld by them, enveloped by them.

And then the vision ended. Just like that. In an instant it was over. Sound returned: traffic in the distance, a siren, a horn honking. The wind resumed its cold movement over the roof. The gray sky spread out over me like a blanket and the crow suddenly spread its wings and launched itself into a wide arc over my rooftop and out into the world. As for me, I stood motionless for a time, a little bewildered. I was not really sure what to think or what to do. I had to just be still and take it all in. What had just happened? Was it real? It took me a while to re-enter my reality. The gyroscope had suddenly stopped spinning, but I needed a moment to clear my head. I looked around me. Same old roof. Same old trees. Same old circle of cornmeal. Same old me. But somehow, everything had changed. And nothing would be "same old" again.

Spiritual vision brings us to a place of decision: do we believe what we have seen or not? Do we acknowledge that we have had a vision, or keep it to ourselves? Do we try to understand how our reality has shifted, or do we doubt that any change has occurred at all? I believe these are questions a great many who are reading these words have already faced. I believe there are more out there who have had spiritual visions than who have not. Some may have decided not to talk about them; some have chosen to talk to only a few close friends or family; some have turned their visions into paintings or poetry; some have been trying to understand the full meaning of vision for their whole lives and, by doing so, have become deeply spiritual persons who have made a great difference in the world.

I did not completely understand what the crow meant by the words she brought to me. At the time, I could only begin to interpret them.

At first the holy words of my vision only brought me a deep feeling of peace. They reassured me that I was not alone in my struggle. Over time they encouraged me to continue following the twin paths of my life as a Christian and as a follower of Native Tradition. I did not fully understand where this balancing act between different cultures would ultimately take me, but at least I knew that abandoning one for the other would be a mistake. As difficult as it might be, I would try to hold them in tension, working with both to find my way to . . . what: Resolution? Reconciliation? Synthesis? I was not sure, but I was willing to do what the vision told me and remain patient. I was awed enough by what I had experienced to be shocked into a level of belief that let me move forward with my life.

In the years to come, I found walking this bicultural road to be very difficult. I came to appreciate how being patient was not simply a matter of sitting in God's waiting room, but a serious test of faith. Many times I was tempted to let go of my Christian faith to simplify my life as a Native American. At times this dual path caused me to be in a spiritual limbo. I used to say that I was too white for Indians and too Indian for whites. I felt like I did not fit. I lived in the tension between cultures, trying to remain faithful to both Native tradition and Christian teachings.

Consequently, my vision was an ongoing mystery. It did not give me instant gratification, but only helped me to see through a glass but darkly. I believe this was an important part of my vision because so often in contemporary American culture we want immediate answers to our questions. The crow did not give me a resolution to my conflict, but only a test of faith. My transformation, therefore, was a process, not a solution. I continued for the rest of my seminary education trying to balance my Christian life with my Native history. It was a difficult exercise in ambiguity, but looking back I recognize that true understanding develops over time, in the gray areas of our lives, not always in the flash of a single insight. My vision of the crow helped me on my path to leading a spiritual life. It helped to heal me of a deep split that was beginning to tear my mind and heart apart. It showed me that what my own Native ancestors, Choctaw Christians who walked the Trail of Tears, believed was not wrong. It also showed me that there was something else out there waiting for me, something I had to persevere in pursuing, a single path that would one day make sense of my life in ways I could not completely imagine as a young man.

What about you? What did one of your earliest visions look like? When did it come to you? How did it appear? Where were you? What were you doing? Did you recognize it as a vision right away or did you have to grow into it? What images helped you? What words did you hear in a holy voice? What colors were there? What living creatures shared in your experience? How did you carry the vision with you?

There are a thousand questions I would like to ask you. And there are a thousand ways you can answer as you tell me about your vision, about what it has meant, about how it has changed your life. And I believe, although the world may have always known you by a single name, the truth is you have been given many names. You have changed, been changed, and emerged from the dreamtime of vision to discover yourself anew.

I want to be spiritually bold enough in this book to claim this territory of integrity for all of us who have received a vision in our lives. I want to do so to stake out our space, our story, in the realm of the religious. I do not do this only for any group of us, but for all of us, whether we are Christian or not, whether we are Native or not, whether we are religious or not. I believe there are no fences we can build around the vision of God to contain it or explain it. Instead, I think vision is a wild truth. It appears as it will to whomever it will. It arises in many different forms to many different people of many different walks of life. It has come to you, to me, and to countless others through the centuries.

Vision is not a private club for the initiated few, but a wide spiritual sea on which any person may sail. You and I discovered that fact, and we are not alone. Many others were alongside us, even if we could not see them, or hear their story, or understand their experience. Like ships passing in the night, we may have missed many chances to realize just how full of mystery our lives are. We may have felt hindered by our own cultural and religious training from sending out signals into that night, openly sharing our own visions with others for fear of rejection. Therefore, we have sailed alone and we have sailed in silence.

That is something we must change.

Vine Deloria was right when he said that a story like *Black Elk Speaks* would be like water in a desert. He described our historical period very accurately. We do live in a time when vision is few and far between, not because vision has disappeared from our lives, but because we have been conditioned not to embrace it or speak of it. We have entered the silence of the cultural void that Vine describes, an age where celebrity passes for the heroic and the constant sensations flashed before us on screens fail to reach any deeper in us than entertainment. We live in what he called "that strange isolation."[23]

Vision can break that spell. It can release us from our isolation. Not because it is magic, but because it is so human. When we reclaim the ancient human experience of receiving spiritual vision, when we openly acknowledge that we live in a world of deep mystery, when we tell our stories to one another, when we are able to celebrate the fact that even the most ordinary person can be shaped by the most extraordinary encounters, then we can shatter the silence of an age that sits before a screen and waits for digital data to tell it what is real.

If I speak openly of my own humble vision and ask you directly about yours, I do so with a purpose. My intent in this book is not only to convey a Native American approach to the study of Jesus, but to invite my readers into an insurrection. I seek to solicit each of you into the subversion of spiritual silence. I want you to join me in honoring the vision that has helped to shape your life. I encourage you to be bold in claiming these visions and, more than that, in finding ways to share them with others. I do so because I believe the more we can open the dialogue of visionary experience, the more we can discover the deep bonds of our common humanity.

God has not spoken only to a handful of us. God has not spoken only to the few. The whole reason for the Incarnation is so that God could enter into the vision quest and speak to us all. The experience God had as a human being is the same experience you and I have as human beings: We enter the world of vision. We see and hear in a new way. We understand more deeply. We are transformed. The borders of our sacred space are widened; we open up to an awareness of new possibilities. Vision does not take away the struggles of our existence, but it does show us how to cope with those struggles with confidence and hope.

My first vision was small: a single bird, a single message, all in a single moment. I walked out alone to make my lament many years ago. I was a deeply troubled young man who felt that he had to choose between two parts of himself. I was coming apart spiritually. I cried to God to help me understand. I saw a vision. I heard a holy voice. Afterward, I felt whole and I had a sense of direction. On the surface this simple narrative may not seem that important, but stop to consider the wonder it reveals. With a single image, a fragment of vision, a brief word, God was able to overcome generations of suspicion.

When I stepped out onto that roof, my ancestors stepped out with me. The whole long history of their struggle, survival, and spirituality was in my mind and heart. My lament was more than a question about my own doubts; it was a question about the integrity of my culture. Memories of racism, genocide, exploitation, and humiliation stood with me in that circle of cornmeal. Issues of the identity of God, the truth of the Bible, the authenticity of tribal traditions were all there as well. In myself, I may have been no one special, but like every human being I embodied the sum of my life story. I carried the cultural baggage of my birth. As a Choctaw, I carried the Trail of Tears with me. Knowing whether or not Jesus made that walk with my ancestors was of enormous consequence. The epiphany of the crow came into the heart of this torn spiritual reality and began the process of healing it. Not instantly. Not easily. But with authority. With power.

When we assert the validity of our visions, as humble as they may be, we acknowledge the power of God to change reality. We acknowledge transformation. We acknowledge that there is no history, whether personal or corporate, no matter how painful or distorted, that cannot be redeemed by God's intervention. In an age such as the one in which we live where both individuals and cultures are so isolated, there are few messages of hope more important than the one we can announce by speaking of our visions.

There is a poignant comment that Black Elk makes when he is explaining to John Neihardt why he is willing to have his vision recorded:

> *I am going to tell you the story of my life; and if it was only the story of my life I think I would not tell it; for what is one man that he should make so much of his winters, even when they bend him like the snow? So many other men have lived and shall live that story, to be grass upon the hills . . . This then is not the tale of a great hunter or a great warrior, or of a great traveler . . . So also have many others done, and better than I. But now that I can see it all from a lonely hilltop, I know that it was the story of a mighty vision given to a man too weak to use it; of a holy tree that should have flourished in a people's heart with flowers and singing birds, and now is withered; and of a people's dream that died in a bloody snow.*[24]

Like Black Elk, you and I are ordinary people with no special claim to God's grace or insight. And like him, we have also been given the opportunity to make our lament, to go crying for the vision that will shape our lives, and perhaps help to shape the lives of many others. The sadness of Black Elk's confession – that he believed he had been given a mighty vision but that it was "given to a man too weak to use it" – is a haunting reminder of what a visionless world can do. It can break the hope of a nation. It can destroy faith and leave people in a wasteland of sorrow and isolation.

Black Elk's people died in the snow, as did my ancestors when they walked the Trail of Tears. They died because they were captives of a power without vision. They were the prisoners of a system without a Spirit, a soulless machine of greed and racism called colonialism. Today, four decades after my vision, as a man not much younger than Black Elk when he told his own story, I can see clearly. I can see the blood in the snow. I can hear the lament of my people and because of that, I will not be too weak to use my vision for all it is worth. Even if I am only a single person with a small vision to share, I will proclaim it and release its healing power.

I am Choctaw and I am Christian. I have the vision of the Crow. I have walked two paths all my life. I have held the hoop of my faith together. I have come to understand what caused the pain and death that was visited on my nation, and I know that it was not the will of a loving God. The Messiah I knew as a child, the Jesus of my ancestors, walked the long Trail with my people. He was there. He suffered with them. He is not the white man's god, but a Native healer who made his own vision quest, not once, but four times. He went out to make his lament and he was given visions. He was not afraid of the silence. He was not afraid to speak about what he saw and heard and felt, and consequently, he changed the world.

Now you and I are called to do the same. We are like Black Elk. We are like Jesus. We are human, weak and without power. But if we take the risk, if we make the effort, if we claim our own sacred space to invite the vision of God into our lives, we will be transformed. We will receive the wisdom and blessing of God and be given all we need to do our part in rolling back the evil that separates us from one another and from all living things around us.

The Jesus of the Trail of Tears, the Jesus of the Lakota and the Choctaw, the Jesus who went to a lonely hilltop and made his lament is the One who shows us the way. He found his vision, changed his name, and saved his people. He was purified. He was with his trusted friends. He made himself open to the sacred. The more we come to know him, the more we come to understand ourselves. In the end, his vision and ours are intimately connected. His path and ours are one.

Chapter 3

THE VOICE

I heard the voice of God. It came to me one quiet afternoon in a small town in South Dakota. I was sitting in my favorite chair reading the Bible when the voice came to me. It was a voice with which I was familiar because I had heard it some years before when I met a messenger from God on a rooftop.

You have just read the first vision quest of Jesus.

That's what it said. That's all it said. And those few words changed my life.

I had come to North and South Dakota to work for a leadership development ministry with Native American communities in the Episcopal Church. I was a seminary graduate, but had chosen not to be ordained because I did not feel I was spiritually mature enough to become a priest. I had some deep questions to resolve in my heart about being a Native person and a Christian. Being in the Dakotas was a way to work on those questions. My job brought me into close contact with people on many reservations. It gave me a chance to listen and learn from both Christian and Traditional Lakota men and women. As I drove from community to community out across the wide prairie beneath the open sky, I had lots of time to think about what I was hearing and seeing. In the years to come I would often say that seminary was where I did my Western-style graduate studies, but the Dakotas are where I did my Native American graduate training.

I had a lot to learn. Before I settled in the Dakotas, I had traveled throughout the United States and Canada, experiencing life in a wide variety of Native nations. I was the national director for Native American ministries in the Episcopal Church and that role opened a door for me to meet with and learn from indigenous people from every corner of North America and beyond. From Maine to Arizona, Alaska to Alabama, Minnesota to Texas, I crisscrossed the continent engaging with different urban and rural communities. I not only had an opportunity to spend time on reservations and in villages, but I also attended international gatherings with indigenous people from Central and South America, Australia, Aotearoa/New Zealand, Hawaii, Samoa, and Fiji. The breadth of my experience with indigenous people was extensive, but I went to the Dakotas in search of depth. I was following my vision of the crow, searching for a way to live in balance between Native tradition and Christian theology. To do so, I felt that I needed to go deeper. I needed to find the elusive point of fusion between the two. I thought I might find it where the spirit of Sitting Bull and Crazy Horse still watched over the land.

I was searching for an authentic way to be both a Native American and a Christian. I wanted to understand how to live a spiritual life in a traditional Native American way and be a disciple of Jesus Christ at the same time. The path I sought was not separation or syncretism. I did not want to be "bi-spiritual," practicing a bit of Native tradition one day and a bit of Christianity another. I also did not want to gloss one over the other, adding a few feathers to my Christian theology, or following Native tradition with my fingers crossed. I wanted to be able to genuinely live as a traditional Native person, embodying all of the values of my ancestors, practicing the ancient religious sacraments of my people, and do so as a Christian who could say the Nicene Creed without hesitation.

It was something of a tall order. As I traveled around the indigenous world I found that there were lots of Native people who chose one or the other: either they practiced their traditional religion or they went to church. There were many others who were "bi-spiritual," practicing both at different times. But I had not met a Native teacher who could help me see how the two could be brought together without sacrificing the integrity of either. Therefore, I went to the Dakotas to stop chasing the answer. I decided to stay in one place to see if the answer would find me.

In the Dakotas, there were other Native Americans who were Episcopalian like me; the first convocation of these Lakota Christians had begun in 1870 and has continued every year to the present day. There were a large number of Episcopal parishes served by Native American clergy and lay leaders. At the same time, there were many Native people who practiced their traditional faith; there were traditional ceremonies and medicine people to interpret their meaning to me. I thought if I could stop anywhere to wait for enlightenment, the Dakotas would be a good place. For a young Native man wanting to understand how to live in two worlds at once, this was the place to be.

The irony is I did find what I was looking for, but not in the place I expected. In my romantic imagination, I believed I would find my answer in a religious ritual or ceremony, either Christian or Traditional. I thought the answer might come to me high on a hill doing a vision quest, in the womb-like darkness of a Sweat Lodge, or in a camp meeting out on the prairie. The vision I had from God had been a little like that; it had surprised me during my ritual of morning prayers in Cambridge. But in the end, the answer found me sitting in a chair. I had been reading the gospel according to Matthew, letting the familiar words of his story slip through my mind like a gentle stream, when suddenly the holy voice I had first heard on the rooftop returned and shook me awake in my spirit.

You have just read the first vision quest of Jesus.

I smile now because I can remember scrambling to come awake when those words caught me off guard. I consider this voice to be from God because it appears from some place other than my own consciousness. It announces itself. It speaks in a clear, simple, uncomplicated way.

When I have attempted to explain this experience to others I have often laughed at myself because the voice I hear sounds as if it is speaking to a small child. I do not receive long and elaborate messages from God, probably because God is not sure I could understand them. Instead, I get the brief, direct words needed by a prophet with a short attention span. One of my images of God is that of Grandmother, the wise old Native woman with gray hair and eyes as ancient as the Earth. She takes my face gently in her hands and holds me in Her gaze as She tells me what She thinks I need to know, forming the words slowly so I can remember them and let them sink in.

I embrace this feminine image in the same way Hebrew tradition refers to the voice of God as the bat kol, the daughter of the voice. It is that mysterious presence that comes from some source beyond, a communication that defies our ability to categorize. Therefore, like the theologians of ancient Israel, I give the voice a female personification because I experience it in that way.

I suspect many, if not most, of us are more than a little shy about admitting we hear "voices." When I was a postulant for Holy Orders (a person being screened to see if he or she is a suitable candidate for ordination) I remember laughing with my peers about the psychiatric examination required in the process. Part of that examination was a series of written questions that had to be answered yes or no – among them were questions such as, "do you hear voices?" Any sane person, or at least anyone sane enough to understand what it would mean to the psychiatrist if you replied yes, would check off no. But the choice can be an odd one for people who believe they have a call from God to become ordained. Men and women preparing for seminary are usually fairly well versed in the Bible, and in that book there are numerous examples of human beings hearing the voice of God. There are messengers, angels moving back and forth from Earth to heaven, carrying instructions to faithful men and women, people like Samuel who heard the voice call his name, and Mary whose response to the voice became enshrined as The Magnificat. So checking off a no to the question about hearing the voice of God becomes something of a joke. It bows to the conventions of our society where hearing "voices" has a negative meaning, but it also reminds us that we come from a religious culture that historically has expected this kind of an exchange to be possible.

If you come from both a Christian and a Native American background then you are doubly likely to accept the reality of the voice of God being real because Native American tradition is also full of stories of communication between the realm of the divine and the world of humanity. The Native American religious tradition in North America accepts the idea of close contact between God and human beings through the agency of many spirits who carry the divine message with them. These spirits are not phantoms, but are most often seen as living creatures in the natural world chosen to bring the sacred word. Buffalo, bear, eagle, raven: many creatures can be conduits for the voice of God.

What happened to me that afternoon in South Dakota, therefore, is not something so strange when seen from the perspective of ancient Christian and Native American spirituality. In fact, I believe it is quite common. I believe many people hear the voice of God, even those who try not to hear it. We hear it because we need to hear it, because without it we cannot find the transformation we need.

I needed to hear the voice. I had been waiting for it for years. My odyssey through so many indigenous communities had been a continuation of the quest that had begun years before when I received a vision from God. Over time I came to realize it was leading me to find a spiritual path that would unify Christianity and Native American tradition. Until I could do that, I would never rest easy in my life. Like a lost piece to my own puzzle I would never find a sense of being whole. I needed to hear the voice of God, to receive the wisdom of God, to help me discover what I could not find alone. That is what I said to my bishop when I told him I could not be ordained. After three years in seminary, on the threshold of ordination as a priest in the church, I informed my bishop that I could not go forward because I was not ready. I was incomplete. I was Native American and Christian, but I was not sure what that meant. I remember explaining to the bishop that in the Native way a person cannot become a "holy man" or "holy woman" just by going to school for a few years. Sometimes it takes a lifetime. It takes the slow work of a whole community, affirming and supporting the development of that person; it takes mentors and teachers, especially the elders who can show the person how to live in a sacred way.

I told the bishop I had received a vision and had to honor it. I had to wait. I had to find myself, my whole self, before I could even consider being ordained. My bishop was a good man. He understood and supported me. He released me from my commitment to become a priest and prayed me on my way to find what I was seeking. I remember hanging up the phone after speaking to him. I remember sitting there wondering what to do next. I had just stepped off the path I had been following from childhood, the path my grandfather and great-grandfather had both followed to ordination, the path I thought God had called me to take to find my vocation. I thought I knew what God wanted from me when I started seminary, but after my vision on the roof all I could do was trust the voice.

The voice of God is vision internalized. It is not what we see outside of ourselves, but what we hear within ourselves. The crow that I saw in my vision was a messenger of God. The voice I heard was the message itself.

The challenge of the vision quest is not only to believe what you see, but trust what you hear. Trust is the fulcrum of faith. To believe is to trust. Spiritual truths are not scientific truths. We cannot put hope in a test tube or compassion under a microscope. In the end, what we believe is what we trust, even if there is no tangible evidence that can guarantee that our faith is well placed.

One of the fundamental differences between European and Native cultures is how they understand trust as a spiritual value. When I was a seminary professor I would tell my students that the easiest way to express this difference is to say that white people want to see the data and read the fine print before they commit themselves to believe something. In other words, their motto is, "I will believe it when I see it." On the other hand, Native Americans assume that only an experiential encounter with the holy can reveal the truth. They follow the motto, "you will never see it if you don't believe it."

Reading the gospels in the Native American context, Jesus confirmed this traditional attitude on more than one occasion. When he is about to raise Lazarus from the dead, he says to Martha: "Did I not tell you that if you believed you would see the glory of God?"[1] When

Thomas cannot believe that Jesus himself has risen from the dead, Jesus says to him, "Because you have seen me you have believed; blessed are those who have not seen and yet believed."[2]

Seeing and believing are the essence of a vision quest. They operate in the process of trust. We create faith each time we are willing to step out onto the ice of God's word. When the voice of God told me to be patient, I had a choice to accept that word on trust or not. When the voice returned to tell me that I had just read the first vision quest of Jesus, I had the option to accept that idea or ignore it. There was no proof in the beginning of my quest that if I remained patient I would discover the path the crow had shown me in my rooftop vision. There was no guarantee that if I heard a voice speaking to me in South Dakota that it was telling me the truth. The connecting point between what I thought I saw and what I thought I heard was faith. Either I believed it or not. The choice was mine.

The spiritual glue that held the Native community together around the Native Covenant was not doctrine or dogma as much as trust. The value of telling the truth was one of the first virtues Europeans commented on when they encountered Native people. In traditional societies a person's word was more than their bond; it was their religious identity. Without truth there could be no trust; without trust there could be no belief; without belief there could be no faith; without faith there could be no community. Therefore, the truth claim of Native religion is not contained in a creed, but in a behavior.

Red Jacket's famous response to a Christian missionary is one of the best known examples of this spiritual principle in Native tradition. Red Jacket was a leader of the Seneca nation. In 1805, when his people were asked to convert to Christianity, Red Jacket turned the "seeing is believing" focus back on the missionaries. He told the missionaries that his people were familiar with white Christians because some of them lived nearby the Seneca nation. He said that his people would wait a while and observe these Christians. If the Christian religion did what it claimed to do, if it made these Europeans less likely to cheat Native Americans or take their land, then Red Jacket's people would seriously consider adopting the white religion.[3]

This story finds an echo in the gospel stories about Jesus. When the followers of John the Baptist come to Jesus to ask him if he really is the Messiah, Jesus says that they should go and tell John "what you have seen and heard."[4] The truth claim is contained in the action: Jesus heals the sick and brings comfort to the poor. He does what he says. His words and his actions correspond. We can believe in him because we can believe in what we have seen and heard him do.

The real issue, therefore, from the Native American viewpoint is do we trust ourselves? Spiritually speaking, if we are balancing our trust on what we see and hear, then how much trust do we have in our own perceptions?

When I went out on my first vision quest, I was not sure I could trust myself anymore. I was not sure I could trust what I had heard or seen. I had doubts about my perceptions of both history and religion. I needed a different perspective, a confirmation of a truth in which I could believe. The "proof" I needed could not be found in classrooms or books alone. The reason I told my bishop that I was not ready to become a priest was precisely because of this gap between what I saw and what I believed.

In the Dakotas I began to find a different kind of truth claim. Religion is not a rule but a relationship. It is, as Jesus tells us, the relationships we have with God, with one another, and with ourselves. The purpose of the vision quest is to keep these relationships in balance and it does so by working directly on the seeker's own perceptions of his or her self-worth.

The vision quest is how Native people go to Confession.

As we have seen, Native Americans do not approach the quest in a heroic posture. They go, as Kierkegaard would say "with much fear and trembling."[5] The person coming in humility before God begins with a recognition of his or her own imperfection. There is an admission to be made in the lament, a clear expression of the condition of the human being as not being able to see clearly, not being able to hear wisdom in the world around them, not doing what they think God would want them to do.

When a Native person steps into a circle to perform the classic vision quest, he or she steps into a spotlight. The person's flaws are as visible as his or her strengths. The crying out to God is much like an infant would cry to their parent for attention. It is predicated on the confession that as human beings we are vulnerable and need help. It reflects a spiritual admission that we are creatures who do not clearly see or understand our own reality, and therefore, are more than capable of making mistakes. While the term "sin" may not be used as heavy-handedly as it is in Christian theology, the implications that human beings are imperfect, thoughtless, and potentially hurtful to other life forms is apparent. Like children we may be innocent, but we can also be very cruel.

The vision quest is an instrument of reconciliation. It begins with an admission of brokenness. However, it does not suggest that human fragility can be overcome through the acquisition of power or secret knowledge. Very often non-Native persons who have commercialized the vision quest as part of their manufactured spirituality present it as a method for achieving personal power. They talk about "power animals" that will give a magical name to the person and allow him or her to have access to higher levels of consciousness. This kind of commercialization of Native American tradition totally distorts the real vision quest because it bypasses the confessional nature of the quest and it targets personal gain rather than reconciliation.

Forgiveness is not quite the right word to describe the Native theology of reconciliation. Without an original sin to be redeemed, Native theology looks more to the restoration of an unbalanced relationship. When a Native person undertakes the traditional vision quest he or she is lamenting the loss of relationship with God, not because of sin but because of a breakdown in the see and believe process. The vision that the person is seeking is a tool for restoring this balance. In both Christianity and Native tradition, reconciliation is right relationship. The classic vision quest for Native people is the effort to receive the right spiritual prescription to heal relationships that may have gotten out of alignment. Therefore, Native people speak in terms of the vision quest as being a source for "good medicine."

Once again, there can be some confusion when this concept of spiritual medicine is translated into the European paradigm. It can sound like magic. The healing power Native people receive from a vision quest has nothing to do with magic. It is not a formula for arcane practices that can manipulate reality. Medicine is closer in meaning to blessing or benediction. Through a vision quest, the Native man or woman is shown how they may become an agent of blessing. They are given insight into how they may so reconcile their own life in balance with God that they become a source of this same healing for others. They may be given a special song that embodies this blessing, knowledge of a particular herb or powder that may anoint persons with healing power, or actions they should continue as their quest carries on into areas of even deeper awareness.

None of these things are, in and of themselves, magical. They are liturgical or sacramental, just in the same way Christians would use those words. The good medicine of Native American theology, therefore, is not that different from the good news of the Christian experience. Both traditions understand how a spiritual power can be transmitted through natural elements (e.g., the oil of anointing for Christians or the smoke of healing for Native Americans). By themselves, these objects have no inherent magical powers, but when used in alignment with a spiritual intention, when used as blessing or unction, they take on the role of dynamic agent for the purposes of God through human action.

In my own vision, everything that I have just described took place. I began my quest with a lament, a confession of my own ignorance and weakness. I received the grace of reconciliation, the ability to come back into balance, both within myself and with all of God's creation. I was challenged to do something for the sake of others. I was commissioned to carry on my quest until I made another discovery. And the whole point and purpose to this activity was to bring some gift of support and healing to others. I did not receive any special powers. I was not singled out because I was in any way gifted as a spiritual person. And I certainly did not understand my actions to be heroic in any sense – in fact, quite the opposite – I thought of myself as being a confused person in need of spiritual direction.

You have just read the first vision quest of Jesus.

When the voice spoke to me again, years after my original vision, what was it telling me? Why was its message so healing? The voice I heard brought good medicine into my world because it helped me comprehend how the Christian tradition and Native American tradition can be reconciled. I had been deeply conflicted for a long time about how I could live authentically as both a Native person and a Christian. I was not alone. Native American communities are still divided between those who practice traditional religion and those who profess Christianity. The two spiritual paths are often seen as being incompatible. The legacy of colonialism still haunts Native America in this way. It has created a kind of spiritual schizophrenia in the lives of people whose ancestors were forced to choose between two faith systems that were presented to them as being mutually exclusive.

The voice told me there is a way to read the Christian scriptures that is in balance with Native tradition. I did not have to choose one or the other.

The passage I had been reading that day in South Dakota was Matthew 4:1–11, the story of Jesus in the Wilderness. The voice I heard gave a name to this passage. It opened my eyes to a new way to read the Jesus story, not just as a Native American convert reading a European story, but as a Christian firmly grounded in my own tradition. In other words, it reconciled Jesus to Native tradition. It revealed Jesus as a Native American.

Understanding this did not happen all at once, of course. At first I just sat in my chair, reading over the Wilderness story, recognizing in it all of the classic elements of a Native American vision quest.

Matthew presents Jesus as going out to a lonely place to make his vision quest. He is going in the spirit of lament, open to being tested and tempted in his weakness as a human being. Jesus sees several powerful visions. He is offered the chance to make these visions about himself, but he stays focused on the good medicine and understands the true power of his vision to heal others. Like any Native person undertaking a vision quest, he is even attended by others who support him. In his case, they were angels who are the spirit helpers so familiar to Native American tradition.

The voice was right: I could read Matthew 4: 1–11 as a Native American vision quest. I did not have to stretch theologically to do so. I did not have to diminish or dismiss any parts of Native tradition to make the story work for me. In fact, by reading the Wilderness account in its Native context, I could discover whole new ways to appreciate it and let it become a source of blessing. I remember the sense of peace that came to me that afternoon. I remember feeling thankful to God for helping me to bring my quest to a close with this wonderful revelation. But the experience was not over all at once. The voice had said "the first vision quest." How many more were there? What else could I discover in the gospels if I kept reading?

The vision quest is not a substitute for life. It is not a one-time other-worldly experience that somehow separates the seeker from reality. In the Native tradition, it is very much a part of everyday life. The voice of God speaks about the good medicine that will heal people in their everyday lives and that will keep on healing them for generations to come. The vision of God shows us how to make our lives better, how to bring the sacred down to earth, how to transform our reality, not escape it.

I knew that if the voice had told me that there were more things to discover I should keep going. A Native American vision quest is not a static thing. It is a journey within a journey. Like a spiral, the visions God grants revolve one into another, insight building on insight, strength going to strength. If God had brought me to this point where Matthew's gospel was beginning to open up to me in a new way, then there must be a reason. I kept reading.

I read the entire gospel straight through. I found the second vision quest. Then the third. Then the fourth and final vision quest. One by one these stories presented themselves to me as the chronicle of a Native American holy man making his vision quests through the course of his lifetime. Each one was different, but each one followed the same sacred pattern of the traditional Native quest, as if the gospel had been written by a Native American author. Jesus was the Messiah of Native America. For me, this was a deep healing.

I found many other parts of Native American theology emerging from my reading that afternoon, not only the four vision quests, but other events and characters in the narrative that took on a Native American reality. In the rest of this book I will try to share some thoughts about the four vision quests of Jesus, but before I do, I want to consider the aftermath of this moment of revelation. The experience I had of the voice while sitting quietly reading the Christian scriptures was the moment when what the crow had told me actually happened – the two paths became one.

The purpose of the vision quest in Native American culture is not to give one person a private audience with God. It is a tool of transformation, a way to help every person become a more spiritually skilled member of the community. By taking my vision with me into the Dakotas, by trusting what the crow had told me and following the twin paths of my life, I had allowed the vision to become a deeper part of me. I continued my quest because I was alert to the lessons I could learn among Native people. I listened. I learned. I lived. Then the message of the crow was ready to be fulfilled.

And yet, in keeping with the nature of the vision quest, the fulfillment was not an end in itself. I had my "eureka" moment, but it was a beginning, not an end. Once I realized that there were four vision quests in the New Testament, the pull of this idea accelerated my desire to learn more. It opened up the Bible to me in a new way. It brought me to a new path of scholarship and service. Only a short while after my discovery, a few of the Lakota elders came to tell me that they thought I should get ordained. They told me that they had been watching me since I had come to live in their community; they had seen how I tried to live; they believed it was time for me to take the step to become a priest. This affirmation came right after the healing I felt when I began to understand the Christian message as an integral part of Native tradition. Up until that point, I had said I would not be ordained because I was too divided in my spirit. Now, the voice had healed me. It had allowed me to unite the twin parts of my soul, my identity as a Native person and my faith as a disciple of Jesus. Without the voice and the blessing of the elders, I could never have been ordained.

That ordination took place at Wakpala, on the Standing Rock Sioux Reservation. It was attended by many Native clergy and laity, by Traditional people as well as Christians. It included a blessing for me not only under the hand of my bishop who ordained me a priest in the church, but also by the sacred pipe, the living symbol of spiritual tradition for Native American people for centuries. The ceremony symbolized the healing. It was the two parts of me being drawn together in a sacred way. It was also a sign that Christianity and Native tradition could be lived together with integrity.

I was not the only person at that service to understand this hopeful message. In fact, within a short time after my ordination a door opened for me to take this message to a different level. I was invited to join the faculty at a major seminary. I began to teach what the voice had brought me to understand. I began to teach Christian theology as it emerges from Native American tradition. I claimed that tradition in a new way; I described it as Native America's Old Testament.

When I first began teaching on the graduate level in the early 1980s I used the term Old Testament to identify the theological nature of Native tradition. The identification was a shorthand way of placing traditional Native American religious teachings into a Christian context, i.e., that these teachings can be seen in a direct relationship to the New Testament in the same way that Christians understand the tradition of ancient Israel. In my classes in those days I would tell students that as a Native American Christian, I had my feet grounded in the Old Testament of my ancestors, with the Old Testament of Israel in one hand and the New Testament of Christians in the other. The image was accurate as a symbol for how my theology had shifted after the voice helped me to find integrity in the different working parts of my spiritual life. My scholarship was based on how these three testaments engaged one another. I came to understand that the experience of ancient Israel and the experience of Native America were similar. They were traditions that encompassed a covenant relationship with God. Both ancient covenants were crucial sources for interpreting the New Testament theologically.

Over time I dropped the use of "old" to refer to these testaments. They are both contemporary living covenants that have their own integrity. Therefore, I speak of the Hebrew Covenant and the Native Covenant to identify these separate, but related traditions. When treated with mutual respect, they can be seen to convey a very similar experience. For example, God had not been the absentee landlord of North America, but had been as active in the life of my ancestors as God was active in ancient Israel. Just as the men and women of the tribes of Israel had come to know and worship the one true God, so had my ancestors. Just as the people of Israel had understood their relationship to God as a covenant, so had my ancestors. Both communities kept a sacred memory of this covenant. These memories were recorded using all of the cultural elements that define a "testament": poetry, prophecy, proverbs, histories, liturgies, and songs. Collected and collated, these many elements form a unified story, a testament. They embody the covenant that a community understands as their relationship to the divine.

The people of ancient Israel were not unique in their religious experience. Like them, my ancestors believed there was one God. Like them, they believed they had been called to be God's people. My ancestors believed they were in a special covenant relationship to God, which is why the names of our North American nations translate into The People. Israel believed a sacred land had been given to them. My ancestors believed a sacred land had been given to them too; they were stewards of this land by virtue of their relationship with God. Israel believed their nation was founded in an exodus, a migration to the "promised land." My ancestors had the same memory of a migration to their promised land. Israel believed God raised up prophets to teach the people. So did my ancestors. Finally, Israel believed that one day a Messiah would appear who would lead them to the next chapter of their sacred history. As we will see later in this book, that is exactly what my ancestors came to believe too.

In the next chapter I will say more about how "messiahship" is understood in the ancient Covenant of Native America. I want to take the time to do that carefully because it is important in making comparisons between Israel and Native America not to conflate their religious experience. Israel developed a monotheistic tradition over centuries; Native America evolved in the same way. The distinctions between the two, the unique ways in which they expressed their covenant relationship with God, requires that they each be accorded their own place in the context of Christian theology.

I need to be clear at this point that I understand that neither Jewish nor Traditional Native religion accepts the idea that Jesus is the "messiah." My purpose is not to expropriate their covenant traditions to suit my own needs as a Christian. However, because I am a Christian, I respect their covenant theologies as deeply formative for my faith in Jesus.

Let me also present my case clearly as a Native Christian: while I understand that the concept of messiahship for both communities is not the same, I believe Jesus is the fulfillment of both the Hebrew Covenant and the Native Covenant. I honor both sacred stories and I believe that they continue in the narrative of Christ. In this way, what I embrace as the "new" covenant of Jesus does not erase either the experience of Israel or Native America, but weaves through these living traditions to confirm them for generations to come. Jesus emerges from the context of the Hebrew Covenant. Jesus also emerges from the Native Covenant.

In doing so, I believe Jesus both corrects and confirms the original covenants God made with God's people. Israel and Native America are not alone in having a sacred memory of the encounter with God. There are many "old testaments." Accepting this broad definition for testaments, the record of any people's experience of God, gives us a much richer understanding of catholicity. As Christians, it means our faith is not catholic because it requires universal adherence to one culture's traditions. Instead, Native American theology suggests that we are catholic because we have a universal respect for the many testaments of world communities. Conversion to a particular tradition, therefore, is a denial of catholicity. It turns universal gospel into parochial piety.

People of every culture and continent have experienced God, sought to understand God, and recorded a memory of God in their sacred stories. Some embrace a monotheistic vision of God, some see a plural reflection of God in creation. As a Christian, I do not denigrate any of these memories since I believe God was present and active in relating to all of humanity throughout history. All I do is make my own profession of faith: that at one point in our shared history God entered into time and space to reveal the purpose of all of our "old testaments."

Within only a short time after the voice spoke to me I was teaching this approach on the seminary level. I was actively introducing this Native American theology into the life of the church. I was able to do so only because good people, both Native and non-Native, both Traditional and Christian, who felt empowered and challenged by the notion of the Native Covenant invited me to teach. I moved from the Dakotas to Minneapolis/St. Paul. I started teaching at a Lutheran seminary and I watched what the voice had created start to take root in Christian theology and grow.

To understand the vision quest and the Messiah to whom it leads, we must first understand the voice of God and the many ways it seeks to communicate with us. God speaks to us all. God seeks us all. Not because we are heroic or unique, but because we are weak and ordinary. We are, all of us, parts of the ancient covenants God has made with our ancestors. There are covenants made with the tribal peoples of every continent and every culture. They are all fulfilled, confirmed, and corrected by the same Messiah in the same way. Each has something important to tell us about the nature of God. They each inform us about the New Covenant.

To deepen our understanding we are all called to undertake our vision quests, just as Jesus did. We are invited to make our lament, to approach God in great humility and even greater hope. We are asked to follow certain disciplines in doing so, to stand before God to make our confession and seek our blessing. The visions we receive are as many and varied as we are, but they all share one thing in common: They are not for our benefit alone, but for the healing, nurture, and enlightenment of our people. Therefore, we learn from one another, we need one another, we are never fully complete without one another. The visions we have are not static or legalistic. They move and grow and change. They call us to step out into a catholicity of covenants.

Jesus followed one of these paths. He was raised in a covenant. He believed he heard the voice of God. He prepared himself as best he could. Then one day he went out to a lonely place to make his vision quest. He was filled with humility. He had no idea where it might end. He was supported by his friends. He learned from each quest and kept going. He lived into the quests set before him by God. He understood them as his role as a healer of others.

Jesus made four vision quests and, by so doing, left us a legacy to follow. Now we are making our quests. We are becoming healers. We are listeners to the voice of God, speaking to us across all time and all history, through many of our own ancestors and the ancestors of other generations, teaching us what we need to know, welcoming us to learn more. The voice is within us, but it is also calling to us. It speaks our language. It knows our heart. If we trust it, we will see visions, and if we see visions, we will live. The people will live.

Chapter 4

THE MESSIAH

On January 1, 1889 a solar eclipse occurred. On that same day a Northern Paiute medicine man had a vision. Like Black Elk, he was taken up to heaven and shown an alternate reality where Native American communities would be at peace. He saw the dead, those thousands of Native people lost to war and disease, brought back to life and living happily in their traditional ways.

Also like Black Elk, he was given instructions for his role as a healer. He was told to return to teach his people to live righteous lives according to the old values. If they did this, he was to tell them that a renaissance would occur where Native nations would be free from fear and allowed to coexist with their white neighbors without further exploitation.

Finally, he was shown a new form of the traditional round dance performed by almost all Native cultures, a liturgical dance that would hasten the coming of all of these promises made by God. The medicine man's name was Wood Cutter, Wovoka in his language. The liturgy he brought back from his vision came to be called The Ghost Dance.[1]

I believe it is difficult for many non-Native people to really understand just how significant Wovoka was in Native American history. His story has become something of a footnote in the recounting of Western expansion. It is usually mentioned in association with the massacre at Wounded Knee, South Dakota, where some two hundred Native people were slaughtered by the United States army in 1890 and dumped into a mass grave.[2] For many historians, this pitiful episode represents the end of any resistance by Native nations against the Western power, the last light of a traditional and sovereign Native presence to be extinguished. The massacre is associated with Wovoka because the elders, women and children machine gunned by the Army at Wounded Knee were followers of his vision. They were practitioners of his Ghost Dance.

To this day, even the few non-Native people who remember Wovoka or Wounded Knee imagine it to be the story of a false messiah who worked up a handful of ignorant followers into an apocalyptic frenzy and then left them to die when the vision failed. Echoes of Jim Jones or David Koresh come to mind. Therefore, the story of the Ghost Dance is relegated to the category of delusion and tragedy. It becomes a morality tale of how religious vision can be exploited and how "weak minded" people can be taken in by false prophets.

In fact, this is exactly the spin on the story that began even before Wounded Knee as local Indian agents, Christian clergy, and military officers quickly branded Wovoka as a huckster. He was presented in newspapers of the day as the Indian who was pretending to be Jesus. After the massacre, he was blamed for inciting pacified Indians into hostile behavior through his promises that they would be invulnerable to the bullets of the Army if they revolted. He was characterized as a charlatan, a second-rate magician, and a mentally unstable fanatic.

Given this long standing prejudice against him, it may seem strange that I would turn to Wovoka as an illustration of how our quest for spiritual vision leads us to Jesus, but the connections are there from the Native American viewpoint. There are lessons to be learned about the meaning of quest, the power of vision, and the ultimate authority of messiahship, if we choose to learn them.

Wovoka was not Jesus, but he is something far more than a false prophet for Native people. He is left in obscurity by his European detractors, but for those of us who honor the traditions of our people he is a clear sign that vision is what makes a people whole, even if they are oppressed—perhaps, especially if they are oppressed.

To put Wovoka into context, imagine the Roman occupation of Israel at the time of Jesus. Then make it ten times worse. Rome occupied Jewish territory with a military presence, but it allowed the puppet government of Herod to remain in place. Jewish religious customs and worship were still permitted. While taxation was outrageous, Jews were still allowed to make their living in ways usual for the time. Their lands and livelihood were not laid waste. Jews were not forced to live in restricted camps as refugees. Their language was not prohibited. Their children were not taken away from them and forced to become Latin speaking copies of Roman citizens.

At the time of Wovoka, the United States occupied Native lands with its military and permitted no form of self-government for Native people. Native religious traditions were outlawed as devil worship and prohibited as forms of sedition. The historic way of life for the people was totally destroyed as the herds of buffalo were intentionally exterminated in their thousands. Native people were placed in the equivalent of concentration camps. Their children were taken away from them and forced into boarding schools where they were only allowed to speak in English.

If the conditions in which people lived during the time of Jesus brought them to long for a Messiah, imagine how deep the longing was for Native Americans at the close of the nineteenth century. In 1889 the Native communities still surviving from Oklahoma to the Dakotas and along the outlands of mountains and deserts from Colorado, Nevada, Utah, Montana, and Wyoming were desperate. The total war and cultural genocide practiced by the white Americans against them had brought them to believe that they would soon follow the buffalo into extinction. And yet, even under penalty of death they attempted to maintain their ancestral religious practices, especially the vision quest and ceremonial dances.

Dancing is liturgy for Native people. It is as integral to worship and community life as the celebration of the Eucharist is to Christian churches. Every aspect of the dance contains rich visionary meaning. The drum is a sacred instrument; the chants are forms of prayer; the clothing worn is like vestments; the movement of the dance is liturgical action that transforms common elements into sacrament. Therefore, Native people sought to carry on their liturgical dances (e.g., the Sun Dance) even though they were forbidden by the white government. Like Christians meeting in the catacombs to secretly share in the Eucharist even at the risk of death, so did the Native faithful gather out of sight of the military to hold their dances. Even if everything else was taken away, they still had this one remaining bond for faith and kinship.

It was not surprising that Wovoka's vision showed him a dance as the centerpiece of renewal for his people. From the Native perspective, that made perfect sense. Dance is the embodiment of the people's faith in God. It is how God is worshipped and glorified. It is the outward and visible sign of the inward and invisible grace that the Creator shows to every tribe and nation. Consequently, once word went out on the grapevine that a prophet had arisen among the Paiute with a new dance that could heal the suffering of the people, representatives from many nations made the long trek to Nevada to see for themselves. They came not out of curiosity, but out of desperation.

Wovoka was a messianic figure for Native Americans in 1889, not because he was a miracle worker, but because he was a choreographer. Native people did not see him as divine, since there is only one God, but they did see him as a divinely inspired visionary who could teach them to do the Ghost Dance. It soon spread like wildfire through many Native nations.

The Ghost Dance, more commonly known among the Native people as The Spirit Dance, was a variation on the traditional "round dance" which is almost generic to all Native communities. This fact alone is significant: a round dance is inclusive. It is not designed to demonstrate the skills of either young men or women. It is not focused on a particular sacramental relationship to the land or other creatures with whom the people are in spiritual kinship (e.g., the buffalo or white-tailed deer). Instead it is a communal dance that draws both men and women, young and old, into the solemn celebration of community.

A round dance embodies community. Like the Eucharist, it is a liturgical exercise designed to demonstrate the bond between human beings and their Maker. Therefore, despite what anxious white people may have thought, the Ghost Dance was not a war dance. It was a "Ghost" Dance because it sought to bring the whole of the community together: the great cloud of witness of the ancestors with the living remnants of the people in the present. It was a "Spirit" Dance because it sought to do this through the medium of a vision quest, a vision quest made not by an individual, but by a whole community.

The Ghost Dance was a vision quest that people could take together. The power of Wovoka's message was that it took the concept of an individual vision quest and made it a communal experience. It drew a sacred circle, the round dance, around a whole community. It allowed people to enter into a shared lament. It gave the Native nations a way to cry before God as they faced genocide. Wovoka's vision was a way for a beleaguered nation to gather in the sanctuary of sacred space to raise a collective lament to God for justice, hope, and healing.

The uniqueness of his Ghost Dance was that the basic elements of a personal vision quest could now be understood as a national experience. First, people had been purified by their suffering. They had sweated blood in their struggle against the white conquerors. They were prepared for the quest. Then they had discovered their wise old medicine man, their mentor, in the person of Wovoka. He helped them to move to a high place where they could offer their lament.

The Dance was this lonely place where the whole nation could go crying for a vision. Wovoka's teachings replicated the vision quest on a large scale, expanding it for all people in their time of greatest need. Given the degree of suffering being endured by so many Native nations under the white occupation, it is little wonder that many of them turned to the Ghost Dance as their last try for salvation. It is also no wonder that this same vision could become lost in translation as the desperation of the people intensified.

During the time of Jesus there were parts of the messianic expectation that took the form of armed resistance to Rome. The Zealots arose from a religious conviction that God sanctioned the use of force against their oppressors. For these men and women, the Messiah was to be more of a war chief than a wounded healer. In a similar way,

Wovoka's message reached many ears with an altered vision. There were Native people who said that the Ghost Dance was a prelude to Armageddon, that the end of days was near, and an angry God would soon visit vengeance upon the godless white oppressors, that there was magic in the name of God which would protect anyone who took up the sword against evil. The zealots of the Tribe of Benjamin and the zealots of the Tribe of the Lakota may have been separated by centuries, but their religious rationale was very much the same.

The spiritual chemistry between a "quest," our longing for meaning, and "vision," our glimpse of meaning, becomes volatile when it is mixed in the medium of "messiahship," that powerful belief that we have found our meaning, especially if we believe we have found it in one person. Those who followed Jim Jones or David Koresh to their own private Armageddon testify to the truth of that volatility. They were consumed by the fires of a quest for vision because they were manipulated by the claims of a false messiah. Others, like the Zealots and Native warriors who wore the "ghost shirt" to protect themselves against bullets, took a religious vision to the extreme. They sacrificed themselves for what they hoped would be true: that they could literally bring the vision out of the intangible and actualize it as a tangible force to alter their reality. They sought to use vision like a sword or a war club.

For every Zealot or Ghost Shirt, however, there were scores of their fellow believers who never saw messiahship as a call to arms. These men and women were oppressed and filled with the lament of their sorrows, but they saw only a vision of hope through the salvation of God. They believed in transformation. Wovoka saw the whole Earth shaken like an old carpet, as if God were doing spring cleaning. The power of the white occupation was broken. The buffalo miraculously returned in their millions. Peace came to the land as people of alien cultures learned to live together at last. Justice was established.

If what he saw were transcribed into the Hebrew culture of Jesus' time it would make sense to the average Judean who longed for the coming of the Messiah. The vision would be a somewhat inexplicable transformation, a great act like the parting of the Red Sea, that would accomplish the purposes of God for the people. How it would happen was not nearly as important as the fact that it would happen and soon. Both Jews and Native Americans lived in this expectation. They saw a similar hope. They longed for a similar Messiah. They also dealt with a similar crisis when it seemed their Messiah had failed. For many Jews of the first century CE, the Messiah never came. They remained in expectation. But for others he did come in the person of Jesus.

As Jesus' teachings spread throughout the hill country outside Jerusalem, many people (the "multitudes" of the gospel stories) came to believe in his vision. He called it the Kingdom of God, the visionary image of a future free from Roman domination when the old traditions and prophecies of their religious past would be restored. Justice would be established. Peace and prosperity would be enjoyed by all. Like Wovoka's testimony, the words of Jesus found quick acceptance by people on the margins. They invested themselves in his vision and anticipated that it would come true in only a short amount of time. When it did not, when Jesus was arrested and killed, the community of the faithful hit a spiritual wall. A great many abandoned the community of Jesus believers. Even the closest of his followers were staggered and uncertain. They remained hidden, unsure of what to think or what to do.

As Christians, we know the miraculous Easter event that revived both the Messiah and the community that followed his vision. We also know that this faith would be tested again under severe Roman persecution when many would abandon the movement again. When Paul went to Rome to be martyred, it was not at all evident that the Jesus community could survive.

The crucible for the volatile mixture of messiahship, therefore, is in the historic experience of the community when it confronts persecution. Martyrdom becomes an icon for this time of testing. Faith in the messiah figure gets stretched to the breaking point. It forces believers to a profound choice: either walk away or stay. There were many moments, both before Easter and after, when people faced this choice as Christians. In exactly the same way, there would be moments for Native Americans who believed in Wovoka's vision to decide to stand or run. In the end, both the Jesus community and the Ghost Dance community faced intense persecution and both came through the ordeal. The Ghost Dance did not fail, even though many of Wovoka's believers were martyred. The vision of Jesus did not fail, even though many of its believers died at the hands of Rome. The true power of the linkage between quest (longing), vision (seeing), and messiahship (believing) is not in its ability to incite the few to martyrdom, but in its ability to gather community, even in the most desperate of days.

By 1890 Wovoka's Ghost Dance had spread throughout many Northern Plains communities. Among them were the Lakota, Black Elk's people. Like many other communities, they had sent representatives to Nevada to learn the dance; they adopted the vision of salvation and began dancing. They did so because the Federal Government had recently ignored another solemn treaty with their nation and taken control of more Lakota land to give to white settlers. The Lakota were to be restricted to small plots of land and forced to become subsistence farmers, even though the areas in which they would live were difficult to farm. To punish the hostile reaction this news caused among the Native people, the white government had further cut any food subsidies to the Lakota. These subsidies were survival rations for the people since the Americans had been following a scorched earth policy articulated by General William Tecumseh Sherman to eradicate their food source.[3] By this date millions of buffalo had been systematically slaughtered.

Weakened from hunger and stripped of their dignity as hunters, small bands of the Lakota gathered to perform the Ghost Dance as a last hope for redemption from what they saw as genocidal oppression. On the Pine Ridge area in the southwest corner of the Dakotas, one of these bands under the leadership of an elder, Big Foot, decided to travel to be with their kinsfolk. The 7th Cavalry, the same military force that had been defeated at the Battle of the Little Big Horn under the command of George Armstrong Custer in 1876, intercepted Big

Foot's band and told them they could not move because even travel was restricted for Indians.

Under the command of Col. James W. Forsyth, the 7th Cavalry positioned Hotchkiss guns, the late nineteenth century version of machine guns, around the Lakota camp. Tensions were high because only two weeks earlier the most revered medicine man of the Lakota People, Sitting Bull, had been killed by government police when they attempted to arrest him for no other reason than a fear of what the Ghost Dance might be doing to incite the Native people into some action. The death of Sitting Bull, shot under mysterious circumstances, had left a shroud over the Lakota's hopes. In turn, the soldiers of the 7th Cavalry were anxious to avenge their historic defeat at the hands of the Cheyenne, Arapaho, and Lakota alliance that had beaten them before. What happened at a place called Wounded Knee on December 29, 1890 was their chance.

Col. Forsyth ordered his men to disarm the few Lakota men who were part of Big Foot's band; most were elders, women, and children. Without their rifles these men could not even hope to hunt for rabbits to feed their families, so they resisted the order. The 7th Cavalry opened fire. In the words of the man sent out by the Smithsonian to survey the "battlefield" and interview the few Native survivors:

> At the first volley the Hotchkiss guns trained on the camp opened fire and sent a storm of shells and bullets among the women and children . . . The guns poured in 2-pound explosive shells at the rate of nearly fifty per minute, mowing down everything alive . . . the surviving handful of Indians were flying in wild panic to the shelter of the ravine, pursued by hundreds of maddened soldiers and followed up by a raking fire from the Hotchkiss guns, which had been moved into position to sweep the ravine.[4]

The corpses of some two hundred Lakota people were piled up and then placed into a mass grave; photographs were taken to commemorate the "victory." To add insult to injury for this massacre, and perhaps to send a clear message to any other Native people who dared to disobey an order from the white authority, around twenty soldiers who participated in the slaughter were awarded the Congressional Medal of Honor, the highest medal for bravery given by the United States.[5] At Wounded Knee in 1890 a military force gunned down innocent civilians in a massacre. They killed the dancers, but they could not kill the Dance.

The spirit of the Ghost Dance survived because the people's longing for redemption survived. Their envisioning of a day of justice and their faith in God survived. The dance moved into the hearts of the people. Even though they were penned up in cages called reservations and denied the dignity of their own culture, they did not submit. They continued the vision quest, only this time, not just individually, but collectively, as Wovoka had showed them. They kept the vision of nationhood alive. They maintained their belief in their traditions. They spoke their language in secret, but they spoke it.

What we learn from Wovoka's vision is that the same impulse that brought early Jewish converts to Christianity brought Native Americans to the Ghost Dance. It also kept them faithful to that vision, even when the price for doing so became a matter of life and death. Although the historic context of the two movements is very different, a comparison of early Christianity and the Ghost Dance has much to teach us about the authority of the vision quest in human life. There is a spiritual magma that increases when people are oppressed, a critical mass of hope that builds up beneath the surface. The outlet for that stress is the messiah figure who can offer a vision of renewal. And once people have taken hold of that vision it is very difficult to take it from them. In other words, the human desire to find fulfillment through the vision quest remains strong within us. It is a desire that transcends cultural and religious histories and, above all, it is a longing to complete the vision quest, not just as a person, but as a people. In this way the experience of the first Christians and the experience of the Ghost Dancers is very much the same. In both cases even martyrdom could not erase the spiritual bond that held them to their vision. The vision quest on which they embarked went deep within them and allowed them to preserve their sense of community, even when it had to survive underground. Early Christians continued their practice of the Eucharist in the catacombs. Ghost Dancers continued their traditions in the hidden corners of the reservations. Both continued to understand themselves as the inheritors of a sacred vision. Their task was to keep it alive, to pass it on, and to keep believing against all odds. Faith in God sustained both communities. Even after their original message bearers, Jesus or Wovoka, were gone, the vision quest continued.

At the turn of the century, Native people were described as the "Vanishing Americans." The aftermath of Wounded Knee convinced the dominant society that Native American tribes would soon wither under enforced assimilation. Their languages would disappear; their culture would melt away; but that did not happen. Traditions that were prohibited continued. Despite a level of oppression that I described as "ten times worse" than what Rome could administer, Native American culture and religion survived. The reason why is hidden in the vision of the Ghost Dance.

A strange little footnote to the story occurred in 1924. A silent movie star, Tim McCoy, brought an old man in his limousine to visit the set of one of his Westerns. The man was Wovoka.[6] Wood Cutter had lived in relative obscurity after the suppression of his dance. He had been reviled in the press and kept under surveillance by the government, but eventually he was no longer deemed a threat. He was left to live out his days as a failed prophet in the Nevada desert. Aficionados of Western history did not forget him entirely, however, and so Wovoka found himself invited to see how Hollywood was recreating the world he and Black Elk knew before it totally vanished.

When Wovoka arrived on location he was a curiosity for the white members of the cast and crew, many of whom would never have even heard of him. However, for the movie "extras," he was a sensation.

Hollywood had hired Arapahos, a Northern Plains nation closely allied to the Lakota and Cheyenne, to play the "bad guys" in the movie.

Historically, Arapahos had been at the Battle of the Little Big Horn and they were followers of the Ghost Dance until it was banned. These men flocked to Wovoka and showed him great respect. The irony of this strange historical snapshot should not be lost on us. For all practical purposes, the Ghost Dance was long gone and buried. The Native American nations were broken and reduced to appearing as extras in the motion picture fantasies of their conquerors. Then quite unexpectedly the original visionary of redemption walks back on stage and astounds his followers. In a flash their old hopes are revived and their memories rekindled.

Wovoka is not Jesus. The Ghost Dance is not the Gospel. Jesus did not appear on the road to Emmaus in a limo. And yet, there is a clue in this odd little story that can bring us to a deeper appreciation of messiahship. The Arapahos did not forget Wovoka, even though his vision seemed to have died. The first Christians did not forget Jesus, even though it seemed he had died. Why? Why would they keep remembering?

I believe a large part of the answer is contained in the vision quest of each man. Consider, for example, that when Black Elk had his great vision, as powerful as it was, it remained his own vision. It was his personal lament. But when Jesus and Wovoka went on their vision quests, they came back with a very different story. Their visions were not just prophecies, but portals. They were visions that invited people who felt broken to step through to another reality where they could be made whole. And even more importantly, this invitation was made to people who otherwise might have felt that they had nothing in common.

The Ghost Dance vision united old enemies. Many of the nations who embraced it had once been hostile to one another. Even within the nations themselves, the Ghost Dance opened the door for people to put aside old animosities and hurts to come together. It was a vision quest that drew in other visions the way a river draws in the many streams that flow into it. The effect is to unify people by giving them a new identity. In other words, Wovoka's vision quest, because it subsumed the vision quests of everyone who joined it, had the power to transform them. It gave them a new name, not just as individuals, but as nations.

For the brief time that it was allowed to be public, the Ghost Dance transformed separate Native nations from fragmented pockets of people into an organic whole. They were no longer just Kiowas, Arapahos, Lakotas, or Cheyenne; they were brothers and sisters of the Dance. They were the Ghost Dance people, the believers in a shared vision of resurrection.

What the 7th Cavalry feared was the same thing Rome feared: that a vision of hope would unite the poor and oppressed into a community with a shared dream. Wovoka offered that vision to people in a dance. Jesus offered it to them in a meal. The Eucharist is the Jesus Ghost Dance. Small bands of Native Americans gathered in secret places to dance. Small bands of Christians gathered in secret places to break bread together. Wovoka embodied his vision in movement; Jesus embodied his in a meal. The Eucharist and the Ghost Dance are brought together in a tangible form that makes the vision of the messiah accessible to a whole community.

Like Wovoka, Jesus experienced the vision quest. He saw a vision that became an invitation for people to claim a new identity, to enter into a new sense of community. Like Wovoka, Jesus offered the promise of justice, healing, and redemption. Like Wovoka, Jesus became the prophetic teacher of a spiritual renewal for the poor and the oppressed. But unlike Wovoka, Jesus was more than just the recipient of a vision or the messenger of a vision. What sets Jesus apart is that he brought the elements of the vision quest together in a way no one else had ever done. Unlike Black Elk or Wovoka, Jesus became his vision.

"This is my body,"[7] he told them. "This is my blood."[8] For him, the culmination of his vision was not just the messiahship of believing in him as a prophet. Through the Eucharist, Jesus was not just offering people a chance to see his vision, but to become a part of it by becoming a part of him. Native people believed in Wovoka; they believed in his vision; they believed in his dance. In this way, he was the Messiah of their longing, but in doing the Ghost Dance they did not believe they were becoming part of Wovoka. He always stood apart. He was the messenger, not the message itself.

In the Eucharist, however, as it is understood by those communities in the church who see it as more than just a symbolic memorial, Christians believe they are in the actual presence of Jesus, that they are literally bringing him into themselves, becoming part of his "body." The messenger and the message become one in the same. The vision and the visionary are physically joined. The accessibility of the vision is made tangible; you can literally hold it in your hand.

This kind of vision quest is far beyond what Native American tradition understood. It was also far beyond what Jewish tradition understood. The scandal of the Eucharist is that it not only represents Jesus as God incarnate, but it allows human beings to touch God. This thought drove many people away from the Jesus community. It was a vision of messiahship that went to a place many people simply could not go. In both Jewish tradition and Native American tradition a Messiah figure could be several things (a visionary, a prophet, a war leader, a teacher), but not the Creator of the entire universe sitting next to you at dinner. The intimacy of that concept short circuits our almost primal thoughts about the distance between God and humanity. It can seem obscene, and certainly for those who persecuted the earliest Christians it was excuse enough for branding them as religiously perverted.

Even today, many people find it impossible to embrace the messiahship of Jesus as the literal incarnation of God. They prefer to treat him like Wovoka, either accepting him as a well-meaning prophetic visionary or rejecting him as a delusional fanatic. Either way, the messiahship of Jesus remains firmly grounded in his identity as a human being. The radical Christian assertion that he is more than this, that he is a vision quest come to life, God in human form, is the quantum leap of faith that takes Jesus from Messiah to Christ. To take that leap we must accept Jesus not only as the messenger, but as the message itself. We must believe that what the human being, Jesus, experienced in his life was a spiritual quest so powerful that it could only have been taken by God. Therefore, God and Jesus are the same. They have the same name. In order to believe this, we need to do for Jesus what we have done for Black Elk and for Wovoka: we need to consider his vision. We need to understand what he saw. As much as we can, we need to enter into the quest with him and try to see the vision he experienced. Then we can come to the place of decision where we can decide whether we believe this is the God quest, the Christ vision, the thin place where God became human and dwelt among us.

There are, of course, many different ways we can approach the Jesus story. We have the whole of the New Testament to explore in trying to understand Jesus and we have centuries of European church history to tell us what it all means. But I would like to offer a different path, one that begins in the ancient traditions of Native America and that takes us through the mystery of the vision quest to find the Christ we are seeking. If, in fact, the Jewish rabbi, Jesus of the first century, is truly the Christ of the twenty-first century, then he must be transcendent of time and culture. He must be as much a part of the Native story as he is of the story of any tribe or people. Consequently, we should be able to see his vision through the lenses of Native American tradition as clearly as through European thought.

Accepting this viewpoint gives us a place to start. It positions us in the context of the Native American understanding of a vision quest. It says that we can open up the New Testament and begin to read it as if it were emerging directly from the history, culture, and spirituality of Native America. Jesus, therefore, becomes a Native American Messiah, a spiritual figure clothed in the religious outlook of the indigenous people of the Western Hemisphere. Although the events and characters mentioned in his story were originally people of Israel under the Roman occupation, they can be translated into Native people under the American occupation. As we try to imagine the vision of the Christ, the universal Messiah of all people, we start to see Jesus as an Arapaho, a Cheyenne, a Paiute.

What does the New Testament look like if it is seen as the Jesus story that arises from the "old testament" of Native America? It tells us that the Native Messiah, Jesus, went on four sacred vision quests. Four times he was purified. Four times he was accompanied by his friends to a lonely place. Four times he made his lament. Four times he received a sacred vision. Four times he showed us how his name would be changed, and because of that, how we would be changed too.

The four vision quests of Jesus are the cardinal points on the compass of Christology. They each tell us something important about the person and the message of Jesus. Moreover, they tell us these things in a Native American way. They help us to make new discoveries about who Jesus is as a spiritual teacher emerging from the heart of Native American tradition.

The words are unchanged from the gospel narrative with which we are familiar, but the voice is different. It is the voice of a great and wise medicine person, a holy person of Native tradition, who has returned from the quest to share a vision that will transform and heal us.

This medicine person is neither male nor female, neither Arapaho nor Cree, Apache nor Ojibwe, but the embodiment of all Native people, a bearer of our shared longing and hope. Our search for the Christ in Native spiritual tradition opens up our ability to read the New Testament from a perspective that is respectful of and inclusive of all Native American communities.

Therefore, we will find the echoes of different Native religious teachings in the vision quests of Jesus. There will be some of the Longhouse tradition of the woodland peoples, the Kiva traditions of the desert peoples, the Sun Dance traditions of the Plains peoples. Just as the New Testament itself is a many layered story of and about Jesus, with a wide number of different cultures and classes of people included, so is the Native American reading of that story inclusive of a variety of communities.

The common thread that holds it all together is the vision quest. It is the impulse to go find God that has been part of who we are as human beings since the very beginning of our historic journey before we were separated by culture, before we looked different from one another, perhaps even before we spoke a language. Millennia ago the quest began in tree tops and on savannahs. It began with a few of us looking skyward. It began with some of us lamenting the death of a loved one. It began with a single one of us sitting alone, choosing to be alone, leaving the safety and comfort of the troop, the family, the tribe to set out on a search for something that had no name or definition. The urge to step over the boundaries of what we see to see something we can't see, the desire to understand more deeply why we are here, the feeling that there is another life out there, a mind or a person, a spirit or a presence, greater than us. All of that is the thread of our wondering that winds through human life from before history to the end of our history.

The four vision quests of Jesus are the most critical part of that long search for truth. From the Christian point of view, they are the keys to our search for meaning. From the Native American point of view, they are the visions of the Native Messiah. They are the core of his experience. They describe nothing less than God's vision quest on earth.

They are fundamental to our understanding of Incarnation. Each vision quest is a piece of the puzzle of Christology. They give us a name for Jesus, a way to see how he conceived of his own mission as the Messiah. The four vision quests embody the concept of "messiahship." They show us the fulfillment of the Native Covenant.

Consequently, for all of these reasons, understanding the four vision quests of Jesus is central to the quest of all humankind to find balance with the Creator. These visions are at the center of the circle. They are the Good Medicine for which we have been waiting.

In the end the four vision quests of Jesus will begin a new rhythm in our hearts, a drum beat that will slowly move us to step out into the circle of life, to be close to our sisters and brothers, to pass beneath our ancestors in the land of spirits until we see the vision God has intended for us and learn our new name as God's people, the name our Messiah taught us when his quest and ours became a dance.

Chapter 5

THE CLOWN

What is so funny about John the Baptist? According to the gospel of Matthew, not a lot. In the third chapter we are introduced to John with an attention to detail that almost no other biblical figure receives. We are told what he wore (a camel hair shirt and a leather belt) and what he ate (locusts and wild honey). Not even the Virgin Mary rates such a fashion report, so we know that John must have been someone special.

Matthew tells us that "people went out to him from Jerusalem and all Judea and the whole region of the Jordan."[1] In other words, John drew crowds from both the big city and the country. He was a crossover spiritual celebrity who could reach both the urban and rural audience. What made John so popular was his message. And it was not funny.

Matthew opens the scene by the banks of the Jordon (Matthew 3: 1–11) where John tells a group of dignitaries that they are a "brood of vipers." The Sadducees and the Pharisees were not often grouped together since they disagreed about religious interpretations, but John had no problem insulting them both. He says that even the stones of the earth could be turned into better believers than them. John goes on to deliver a sermon that Matthew records as an example of what brought the people out to listen to him by the riverside:

> The ax is already at the root of the trees, and every tree that does not produce good fruit will be cut down and thrown into the fire. I baptize you with water for repentance. But after me will come one who is more powerful than I, whose sandals I am not fit to carry. He will baptize

you with the Holy Spirit and with fire. His winnowing fork
is in his hand, and he will clear his threshing floor, gathering his wheat into the barn and burning up the chaff
with unquenchable fire.[2]

John uses the word "fire" three times in five sentences, so we get
an idea of why his sermons galvanized the people of his time. He was
an apocalyptic preacher, a prophet of the end of days whose red-hot
images of judgment and retribution must have scared many people
into the water.

They certainly scared me as a little boy growing up in Oklahoma.
I remember hearing evangelical preachers deliver much the same
message. For many years I carried the image of John in my head.
The wild man of the Bible, dressed in camel hair with a long beard,
crying out to the crowd, preaching hell fire and brimstone. It was as
if Matthew had made a movie with words, documenting an unforget-
table character. Through the centuries, other artists have been drawn
to the drama of this striking figure. They have painted John into
icons with fiery red eyes; they have put him into stained glass and
statues; they have acted him out in passion plays and major motion
pictures. John is one of the most recognized biblical figures in the
world. He has become a religious metaphor for divine wrath and
repentance. In contemporary language we could say that John has
gone viral. He is a Bible character few people can forget once they
have encountered Matthew's vision of him. He still draws a crowd.

But why? The funny thing about John is not his message, but his
popularity. After all, John is the only prophet in the whole Bible who
got it all wrong. Even Matthew admits that. In the eleventh chapter
of his gospel, Matthew inserts this amazing little vignette: "When
John heard in prison what Christ was doing, he sent his disciples to
ask him, 'Are you the one to come, or should we expect someone
else?'"[3] John was asking Jesus if he had made a mistake. By the
banks of the Jordon River he had thought of Jesus as "the one," the
Messiah, but now in prison and facing execution, he is not so sure
because of what "Christ was doing." Or, in John's case, not doing.

John had told people that when the Messiah came he would be hacking down the dead wood of humanity. John's fire-filled idea of God on Earth was wrath and retribution, a house cleaning of judgment against sin and disbelief. What Jesus was doing was something entirely different. As the Christ, the expected one, Jesus was telling people to love their enemies and turn the other cheek. Instead of throwing the sinners into lakes of fire, he was having dinner with them. He was not using his winnowing fork to separate human beings into the saved and the damned, but going into the brood of vipers to tell them they were loved.

For John, Jesus must have been an enormous disappointment. Why else would John have sent his own disciples to ask Jesus the question about being "the one?" Therefore, the funny thing is, even by his own admission, John is the one prophet in the Bible whom we should ignore. Without his message of doom and destruction, we see him in a different light. John becomes a character of pathos. He stands flailing his arms by the banks of the Jordon, wearing his outrageous outfit, making much ado about nothing. In short, John comes off looking a little odd, a little strange, even a little funny. And that is exactly the point. We should remember John, not because he was a very good prophet, which he was not, but because he was a very good clown.

To non-Native people this description of one of the great figures of the New Testament may sound terribly offensive. To call John a "clown" seems disrespectful in the extreme. And yet, from the theology of the Native Covenant, it is perfectly accurate because a "clown" in Native American tradition has a different meaning than it carries in European-based cultures. For Native people clowns are not just buffoons whose job is to make us laugh. They are spiritual teachers whose job is to make us think. There are, as always in Native tradition, many variations on the theme. However, we can group sacred clowns into two major categories: the *koshares* of the Southwest and the *heyokas* of the Plains.[4]

The term *koshare* is taken from the Pueblo traditions of the American Southwest. Many Native nations in this area have a spirit figure that appears in dance ceremonies whose role could be described as outrageous or provocative. Sometimes these dancers are painted in broad horizontal stripes of white and black. They may act out during the ceremony, teasing the spectators and participants, even to the point of scatological or sexual innuendo.

The second term, *heyoka*, refers to a Plains tradition of visionary men (to my knowledge this was a vision, like the Sun Dance, that came only to men) who became "contraries"—people who do things backwards. A contrary intentionally does the opposite of what is expected. If it is a summer day, he will wear a buffalo robe. If it is cold outside, he will appear with almost nothing on. This behavior originates during a vision quest and continues for as long as the man feels he has the calling to act in a contrary fashion.

Both the Pueblo dancers and the Plains contraries can be referred to as sacred clowns because their behavior may seem outrageous, but their intention is quite serious. The Native Covenant understands their role as essential to the development of spiritual wisdom. In the case of the *koshares* the sudden appearance of a clown who stands out in the midst of a solemn moment breaks the barriers of convention and has the impact of fracturing the religious perceptions of the participants. This is not the kind of sacred clowning that some contemporary Christian churches include to entertain children. The *koshares* are far different from a Western clown in a red nose and big shoes. With the *koshares* there is a shock value to the spirit embodied by the clown. There is an intentional effort to draw attention through behavior that creates a disorienting presence as unsettling as it is humorous. *Koshares* appear around adult themes of fertility and sexuality. They exhibit our mixed attitudes toward subjects that can make us both aroused and embarrassed at the same time. They are ambivalence personified; they are also raw energy and life.

The *heyoka* also skews the perception of the community, but in a different way. The *heyoka* forces people to pay attention to what is going on not in ceremonial settings but in everyday life. This kind of sacred clown represents the duality that the Native Covenant always seeks to hold in balance. The *heyoka* embodies duality. In other words, when the *heyoka* wears the buffalo robe in summer, the purpose is to remind us that we can never really appreciate what it means to be warm if we do not know what it feels like to be cold. The core spiritual teaching of the dichotomy of opposites is one of the principle functions of the *heyoka*.

Like a *koshare*, John the Baptist stands out in the crowd. He is memorable by both his costume and his behavior. He stays in the mind of all who see him. His presence breaks the normal pattern. His unsettling actions toward the religious hierarchy is shocking. In this way, John, as a sacred clown, introduces an element of chaos into order. This is precisely the theological task of the *koshare*. John invites people to participate in a solemn ceremony, baptism, designed to bring them life. At the same time, he reminds them of imminent death and destruction. The ambivalence, the tension makes us want to shudder in fear and sigh in relief. John mixes our emotions in the same way a *koshare* scrambles reality.

From the theological vantage point of the Native Covenant there are important reasons for this to happen. Native tradition maintains a dynamic understanding of the nature of creation. God has not created a static system, but one that flows and fluctuates according to discernable patterns. The seasons come and go; the sun and moon rise and set. However, within these ordered patterns are unexpected moments of chaos. Rain becomes flash floods; winds create tornadoes. The Native Covenant includes chaos theory in its spiritual equation. Life progresses not only because of constant repetition, but also because it is shocked by energies that cannot be contained. Like sex. Like death.

The *koshare* embodies the chaos of God. It is earthy, seminal, disruptive, and energetic. It weaves through a more stately ceremonial of evolution, like strands of DNA, holding life together, but always capable of producing the unexpected. Sacred clowns are the electric energy that arises when order meets chaos. They are spiritual synapses, firing off the creative power between life and death. They stand in exactly the same place John the Baptist occupies by the banks of the Jordon, with one foot in life and the other in destruction. John's call to repentance is more than a call to change. It is a call to face the reality of existence, the exact point where to be and not to be meet. In Native theology this is the hinge point, the turning point, between life and death. John is the forerunner for Jesus because he stands on this edge. Like a sacred clown, he is a reminder that the power of the sacred can either sweep away the status quo or birth a new reality. John is fully a *koshare* in his appearance and his message. He looks like chaos. He predicts chaos. But he is a sign of hope because he offers the water of life. His actions leave people in a place of uncertainty and expectation, teetering between extremes, which is exactly where a sacred clown wants them to be.

John is also a sacred clown in Native theology because he is so clearly a "contrary," a term in Native tradition that indicates a person who does things in an opposite manner to what is expected. His prophecy is not to be taken literally. It is to be taken counterintuitively. In Native American tradition, if you asked a *heyoka* to walk forward, he would walk backward. If you asked him to stand up, he would sit down. *Heyokas* are funhouse mirrors, they show you the opposite of what you expect to see.

John preaches an angry Messiah who will come to judge human beings and cast sinners into "unquenchable fire."[5] His startling message is so powerful, so graphic, that it offers an unmistakable contrast to the person and message of Jesus. In Native theology, John's role is to paint the background so the figure in the foreground may stand out even more clearly. This is the work of the *heyoka* in traditional Native society. Because spiritual life was understood to be completely interwoven with everyday life, it was important never to take anything for granted. As the *heyoka* walked backward through the community, he was a religious alarm clock, a wake-up call to the community to be ever mindful of spiritual life.

The *heyoka* embodies spiritual mindfulness. The similarities to Buddhist doctrine are intriguing. Like Buddhism, the Native Covenant placed a high value on spiritual awareness. In traditional Native communities even the most mundane activities had spiritual content. There was a Zen-like effort to pay attention to the smallest details of life with careful concentration.

The *heyoka* helped with this by being a visual aide to awareness. The role of the sacred clown is to shake people out of complacency. Their message is to avoid taking life for granted. John's purpose, therefore, is to present his contrast to Jesus as a way to position people for what Japanese Zen would call the moment of *satori*, the moment of awakening.

By showing them how bad things could be, he prepares them for the Jesus vision of how good they can be. Like a *heyoka*, John was grounding spirituality where it belonged, in the everyday life of the people. He was challenging their assumptions, waking them up to see the arrival of a new possibility. Seen through the eyes of the Native Covenant, John does not look so much like a failed prophet after all. His odd behavior and his inability to truly recognize Jesus become understandable. His own calling was to be the sacred clown that prepares the way of the Messiah in the Native tradition of a *koshare* and a *heyoka*. Like a *koshare* John represents the hinge between life and death. Like a *heyoka* he is the contrast between light and dark. In the theology of the Native Covenant, he is essential to maintain the proper balance between the dualities of our earthly existence. We cannot have order without chaos. We cannot have life without death. We cannot have Jesus without John.

John is related to Jesus. In Christian tradition, John is portrayed as the cousin of Jesus, but in Native tradition he would be even more directly related. In many traditional Native cultures he would be seen more as the brother of Jesus.[6] The concept of extended family in Native culture often blurred the distinctions between "cousins," as that term is defined in European families. This filial bond between the two men makes the spiritual relationship even more intense. In Native terms, they share a closeness between them that signifies the inseparability of the opposites they embody. The human story of John and Jesus mirrors their sacred story.

Unpacking this sense of kinship between the two brothers helps to give us a deeper appreciation for their combined religious meaning. For example, given the proximity of their ages they both would have made their vision quests around the same time. It is possible that they shared the same early mentors and teachers. They would have undergone their time of preparation in very much the same way. While we do not read in the New Testament about the vision quest of John, we can make a good guess. John received his call to become a sacred clown with a vision of some of the most powerful spirits in Native tradition. When he came back from his quest, he was a changed man. He may have begun to act in unusual ways within the community, which could explain the odd clothing and diet.

One of the hallmarks of Native tradition as a religious system is its inclusivity. Some religious traditions become exclusive. They have rigid exoskeletons of behavior and they reject people who do not conform. In the Native Covenant there is a far broader sense of inclusion, of kinship for all sorts and conditions of human beings. One of the most striking things about John the Baptist, from the Native American point of view, is he is eccentric. In many polite Christian communities today he probably would have been characterized as a "street person" and discouraged from attending worship. In the Native community he would have been recognized as someone with a unique vision and allowed to behave as he chose.

One of the most powerful messages from John the Baptist is not what he preached, but who he was. In Native theology he is a sacred symbol for our need to be open to the full range of humanity, not the narrow band of our own comfort level. Native communities are eclectic. They are based on the religious assumption that God is the author of diversity; therefore, diversity is holy and necessary. Consequently, the theology of community in Native America accepts the presence of people with differences. As a sacred clown, John celebrates this cardinal virtue of diversity. He represents the radical welcome that Native communities extend to all persons.

He also illustrates how diversity, even to the point of eccentricity, is essential to a healthy spiritual community. John embodies many of the dynamics the Native Covenant would assign to the role of "the Trickster,"[7] a figure not articulated in European-based Christian theologies, although the "old testament" of Europeans contains parallel mythic beings like the Leprechauns.

In Native tradition, the Trickster is most often an animal spirit, especially a coyote or a raven. The role of the Trickster in the Native Covenant is to serve as a spiritual teacher. Stories of the Coyote or the Raven are both humorous and serious at the same time. These spirit-creatures break the rules. They defy social and moral conventions. They try to get away with something. The results are sometimes calamitous, but the theological teaching is always clear. The Trickster underlines spiritual wisdom. Like a contrary, the Trickster makes apparent what is underlying in spiritual life. In this sense, John carries on the tradition of the Trickster. He intentionally provokes. He challenges assumptions. He breaks the rules.

Consequently, the Trickster was not always welcome in human society. The Coyote and the Raven were often seen as being on the margins. People were suspicious of their intentions even though the end results often proved to be beneficial. There is a flavor of chaos sprinkled on the Trickster characters, a sense that they are generative forces whose powers may not always be controlled. Therefore, the Trickster figure in Native theology is a recognition that prophetic change never originates within the safe spaces of the status quo. Instead, change begins on the fringes, in the more wild areas of the imagination. John may have returned from his vision quest as a Trickster; he may have been welcomed back into his community as a spiritual eccentric; however, he may also have been too much of a Trickster for his own people to contain.

The missing text in the story of John, from the Native American perspective, is what happened to him after he returned from his vision quest as a sacred clown. Was he out in the wilderness by choice or because his people had exiled him? Did they honor his eccentricity or find it too odd to contain? These questions are echoed in the reaction to John's brother, Jesus. The gospels do tell us about the four vision quests of Jesus, and they also give us hints about how he was accepted by his community. Like John, Jesus returned from his vision quest a changed man. He had a new name.

In his case, the vision he received would have called him to be a medicine man, a healer of the people. But how did his people react to this news? The New Testament gives us many answers, including indications that Jesus was rejected by his home community and driven out of his village. Native American theology pays attention to these issues of kinship and exile because they are so central to the spiritual content of the larger story.

If Jesus and John are exiles, the power of their story takes on a much deeper meaning for Native America. As a community built on acceptance and inclusion, where exile is the very worst form of punishment, the kinship of the two brothers to their clan and nation makes a great deal of difference. If John was an outcast, then as a contrary he would have been presenting Jesus as the alternative: the opposite of rejection. The embodied message of the Native Messiah from the very beginning of the story would have been: no more exiles.

This notion of radical inclusion in the John-Jesus story leads us to consider the fundamental issues of community. Both brothers are intimately connected to the Covenant tradition of Native America. If they were exiles, then this focus on traditional values becomes even more intensified. As a sacred clown and a medicine man, they represent a vision that is special, demanding, and ultimately sacrificial.

The function of the Native vision quest is to show the person making the quest how to give away self to help others. The vision of the sacred clown and the medicine person is doubly demanding. Both clowns and medicine people are the spiritual core of Native community. They embody the traditional virtues to an exemplary degree. Therefore, they must live only for the sake of their people. In some cases, like Sitting Bull, they have to die for the people. By virtue of their vision quests, John and Jesus understand what they are being asked to do. They risk rejection and even exile. They accept that risk for a higher purpose: the ultimate value of kinship. They sacrifice themselves to make a give-away for the good of the people.

Give-away theology is one of the most foundational theologies of the Native Covenant. My ordination as a priest at Wakpala on the Standing Rock Reservation was one of the most important days of my life. After such a long journey searching for how the two paths of my life might become one, it was a celebration not only of affirmation, but healing. The service was held in St. Elizabeth's Church, one of the historic mission churches in the Dakotas. The evening of the ordination the church was crowded with people: other priests and deacons; Traditional and Christian Native people; the bishop; and a medicine person with the sacred pipe. The ceremony marked both my commitment to Christian priesthood and to Native tradition. It was a moment when I received a new name, one that I hold quietly in my heart to this day.

But of all the memories I have of that special occasion, the one I remember most fondly is what happened after the service. All of the people gathered in the parish hall. One by one, my parents, my wife, and I called them forward to receive a gift. My parents had made the long drive from Oklahoma to attend the service. They brought a carload of assorted gifts (blankets, baskets, beadwork) with them to hand out to everyone who was part of my honoring day. Our gifts were only tokens, but they were crucial expressions of kinship. As part of my ordination, I performed the give-away. In Native tradition, when a person is called to a place of honor, they do not receive gifts. They give gifts.[8] This expectation is the reverse of what is common in European-based cultures. To receive gifts would be a focus on the individual, on the "I" instead of the "we." Native people give back to the community on their honoring day to keep the focus on kinship, on the eternal "we" of community.

When I was ordained in the spirit of the Native Covenant, I understood the sacrificial nature of my calling. I made a public witness to that commitment by giving away for the sake of others. While this might be seen as only a gesture on my part, the theological implications for how Native Americans understand the Jesus message are profound.

In European-based interpretations of Christianity, economic justice may be a subject of theory rather than practice. Certainly Latin and Central American liberation theologies saw economic justice in real terms, but in North America the interpretation can be far more muted. However, for Native American theology it is an issue for literal interpretation. Kinship and give-away combine to create a forceful theology of economic justice. In understanding the Native viewpoint, it is important to remember that Jesus talked about money as much as about love. As the Native Messiah, Jesus spoke directly about the need to keep the give-away central to community life.

His messages were not theoretical, but entirely pragmatic. He warned those who withheld what they had from the give-away that they would not find eternal life. He blessed those who gave what they had, even if it was very little. He connected discipleship to stewardship. He told his followers that they were to be servants of all. From the Native viewpoint, Jesus was a strong advocate for keeping the bonds of kinship real through the actual distribution of wealth. To recognize how powerful that concept is in Native theology, imagine the CEOs of American corporations celebrating their rise to the top of the corporate ladder by giving away their wealth to the workers in the company.

Native American Christian theology is unambiguous in its call to economic justice. Ideas like fair housing, adequate health care, and the rights of all working people are not sentimental hopes in the Native Covenant. They are clear responsibilities. They represent kinship. Community is not possible without kinship, and therefore, without economic justice.

As the Native Messiah, Jesus expected his followers to live out the give-away in real terms. Social inclusivity and economic justice are the basis for human kinship. There can be no exiles for the Native Messiah. Consequently, there is no equivocation in his teachings about community. In the same spirit, there can be no doubt that the Native Messiah called us to account for our give-away relationship to all other living creatures in the greater network of our kinship. One of the hallmarks of the Native Covenant is the simple expression, "all my relations." This phrase is often used as an introduction to prayer or public gatherings. It is a verbal icon that symbolically recognizes the presence of all living beings, all created things, in the circle of human kinship. Again, this is not a sentimental expression. It is a witness. It is a spiritual affirmation of both understanding and intent. It means that anyone who follows Jesus as the Native Messiah must be respectful of the matrix of life that encompasses God's great community of creation. Our active commitment, even our sacrifice, to maintain ecological balance with other life forms is expected by God. It is that clear and that simple in Native theology. There can be no exiles. Jesus came to restore balance to all of life, not just to a portion of it.

Because the Creator made everything that exists, and because everything that exists is made in love, the Messiah's call to love encircles all of creation. When we love God with all of our heart, we are loving the Earth. We are loving the seas and the sky. We are loving the four-legged creatures who are our kin, just as we are loving the winged creatures and those who swim. Nothing is outside the circle of love; everything within the circle of love is our relation.

The level of sacrifice that the two brothers, John and Jesus, accepted from their vision quests was a willingness to give away all they had, even their lives, for the sake of the circle of life. John lost his life as a sacred clown because he brought the chaos of hope into the place of power. He spoke the truth. Jesus lost his life because he loved without exclusion. He lived the give-away. Both offer us a clear message. They did not die for symbolism or sentiment. As holy people of the Native Covenant, they expected us to follow them with the same sense of courage and integrity. The give-away they made is unmistakable. The call of the Native Messiah is clear. Our task is not to hold back, not to look for half-measures or loop holes, but to do our part in bringing justice to our community, justice for the tribe of the human beings, justice for all of creation.

If there is still any fire within us, any spark left over from the wild clown by the banks of the Jordon River, let it be our resolve to speak as boldly to the Sadducees and Pharisees of our time as he did: not with a message of sin and retribution, but with the message of the Native Messiah. Let us proclaim the transformative power of love: a love so inclusive that no human being is exiled from its embrace; a love so broad that it touches the life of every creature of this planet; a love so healing that it restores the land and the oceans. Let it be a love without hesitation when it comes to making the give-away.

From the Native American viewpoint, human society will not be able to survive without making the give-away. We are too far gone, as John might have said, in our addiction to power and greed. It is repentance time. Time to turn around. Only a genuine sacrifice will be able to restore us to health. We will have to redistribute wealth where it is needed. We will have to heal our societies from wanting more and rewarding those who take the most. We will need a new system of economic balance and empowerment. It will not be easy. Social and economic justice never are. But if we do not take on this challenge, and soon, then the apocalyptic sermons of John may come true. Except in our case we will be putting the ax to our own tree, cutting down our last hope for environmental and economic sanity.

John was right. We do need to repent. As a sacred clown, he was a sign of chaos in our midst, a reminder of what we might unleash on ourselves if we do not hear the words of the Messiah. His dire predictions warned us of what might happen if we ignore the prophecies we see so clearly in the world around us: poverty, war, ecological ruin. His indictment against the rich and powerful, the comfortable and the complacent, should stir us and move us to turn around and follow the path walked by the Native Messiah: perform the give-away; make kinship a priority; share what you have; take only what you need; honor all living things.

These expectations are the pragmatic teachings of the Native Messiah. They are to be taken literally and lived mindfully. Discipleship, therefore, is community lived in the spirit of "all my relations." It is the sacrifice of self for the sake of the other. A sacred clown and a medicine man have shown us the way. Two brothers died so many will live.

Chapter 6

THE WILDERNESS

No people on earth paid more respect to their dead, than the Choctaws did and still do; or preserved with more affectionate veneration the graves of their ancestors. They were to them as holy relics, the only pledges of their history; hence, accursed was he who should despoil the dead.

Horatio Bardwell Cushman, 1899[1]

One of the best places to begin a study of the first vision quest of Jesus is in the graveyard – and not just any graveyard, but in the ones still found in some areas of rural Mississippi and Alabama. The gravesites are like small mounds overgrown with grass, trees, and vines. They are hard to identify because they blend into the natural surroundings. Some remain intact; others have been plowed up, their contents lost long ago. These little mounds are the graves of my distant ancestors. They are Choctaw burials, usually dating back before the beginning of the nineteenth century CE.

Prior to the arrival of the Christian missionaries, my ancestors would place the bodies of their dead on scaffolds, in a way not dissimilar from the scaffold burials common to many Plains nations.[2] The dead were escorted there by the family as they grieved and then left for a long period until they were almost completely decomposed. Once this natural process had occurred, the family returned to the scaffold with a religious specialist known as a "bone picker" who cleaned the bones and reverently placed them in a box. The boxes of the dead collected by a local community were kept in a special place set apart – a "bone house" – until the holding place was full. Once there were enough boxes of the dead, the whole community carried them to a common place of interment where they were mixed together and covered with earth, creating the small mounds that people honored as the final resting spot for their loved ones.

All of this began to change in the early years of the nineteenth century. Presbyterian missionaries arrived in the Choctaw nation, a geographic area covering most of the current state of Mississippi and extending through other settlements into Alabama, Louisiana, and even Texas. Along with other Native American nations in the southern part of the United States, the Choctaw Nation quickly embraced Christianity. Choctaws, along with Creeks, Cherokees, and Chickasaws found the theology of the new religion easy to adapt.

These Native nations already understood that there was one God. Choctaws understood the story of the Exodus because we have a very similar migration narrative in our own history: long ago two twin brothers led the nation on a long migration to the promised land, *Chahta yakni*, the Choctaw homeland.[3] Like almost every other North American indigenous nation, Choctaws called themselves "the People" in recognition of their covenant with God to be the people of a particular sacred land. Even the Christian story of Jesus as the Messiah made sense to Choctaws. It was not hard for my ancestors to comprehend that humanity needed redemption. After their first contact with Spanish conquistadores, they believed human beings could certainly be in need of salvation.

My Choctaw ancestors had fought Hernando DeSoto as he searched for gold and the fountain of youth.[4] In 1540, they drove him out of their lands, but they understood that these invaders would return. The stories of this alien military power had spread throughout Native American culture. Those nations that had not yet encountered the Europeans had heard about them. They were aware of the technological power of the invaders. They were aware that these people had the use of a new animal that gave them power and mobility: the horse. They were knowledgeable about the intentions of the invaders to control territory for their use in building permanent colonies. It is difficult to summarize how overwhelming this influx of new information was for my ancestors. It would not be an exaggeration to compare their situation to science fiction. It was an invasion by extra-terrestrials. It was a massive paradigm shift.[5]

Like all other Native nations that confronted Europeans, the world-view of my ancestors radically changed. They had a vast array of new cultural contingencies to adapt to and not much time in which to create their strategies for survival. One option, of course, was armed resistance, which was the first response the Choctaws adopted when they attacked DeSoto with such ferocity that the Spaniards retreated from Choctaw land. Within a short time, however, it became clear that armed struggle would not be likely to succeed. Like the Jews of Jesus' time, it was apparent that Rome possessed far more firepower than any other nation on Earth. Open war with the invaders was courting genocide, not that zealots of the Native American tradition did not try. In 1811 a prophet rose up preaching Native American unity and holy war against the whites. He was Tecumseh, a Shawnee visionary and political organizer who tried to convince Native nations that it was not too late to unify and drive the invaders back to the Atlantic.[6]

There were Choctaws who, like many other Native people from different nations, invested themselves in this desperate effort and fought on the side of Tecumseh. However, most Choctaws stepped away from the zealot theology and remained on the sidelines of the conflict. In the end, Tecumseh was defeated and his pan-Indian movement died with him. Looking back, it is hard to imagine how he could have succeeded at this stage in the Europeans' western expansion, given their numbers and the sophistication of their military organization. The lesson to be learned from Tecumseh's brave effort was that some approach to co-existence with the Europeans would have to be found because the dream of eradicating their presence was a forlorn hope. Later in time, war leaders like Crazy Horse and Geronimo would take up the battle, only to be overwhelmed by the sheer might of the United States military-industrial complex. But in the early years of the nineteenth century, the Choctaws shifted to a different strategy.

My ancestors reasoned if they could not beat the Europeans on the battlefield, they would out maneuver them in the fields of culture. Consequently, Choctaws began to study Western ways with diligence. In 1821 they established the first public school system in the nation.[7] They not only learned how to speak English, but more importantly how to read and write it. They adopted Western agricultural technology and began using the printing press. Choctaws had always been organized as a nation state with forms of representative governance, but now they formalized these institutions even more, especially in negotiations with the white government. Councils were held to elect spokespersons to represent the nation under the constant pressure of the Europeans to gain more Choctaw land. Choctaws learned the Western system of laws and court procedures and fought the efforts of white plantation magnates to force them out of their ancient homeland.

During the first two decades of the nineteenth century, the Choctaw nation was able to retain sovereignty, largely due to the sophistication of our people in using Western legal strategies against the Americans themselves. From the Choctaw viewpoint, the ongoing efforts to steal our land were an affront to the honor of the people since it was Choctaw warriors who had stood beside the Americans in the War of 1812. Since we had been allies of the United States, it was even more unconscionable that the white people would turn on us to force us off our land. This insult reached its height when the commander of the forces for whom the Choctaws fought and died, Andrew Jackson, became the president of the United States. He was deeply controversial among his own people. He came into the White House as a populist champion of the western interests of his country, those land grabbers who wanted to drive Native Americans across the Mississippi River in order to use their land for larger plantations and the importation of more black slaves from Africa. The "solution to the Indian problem" was what Jackson offered and once he was in office he took immediate steps to put it into action.[8] He forced negotiations of land treaties on the Cherokee, Choctaw, Creeks and

Chickasaws. The Native American communities, using the Americans' own law, took the issue all the way to the Supreme Court.

They won. In 1832 in the landmark case *Worcester vs. Georgia*, the Supreme Court upheld the legal right of Native American nations to be inviolate in the ownership of their ancestral lands.[9] The Court blocked the effort of Andrew Jackson and his cronies to force Native people out of the southern United States. It looked as if the Constitution of the United States had worked. Native Americans had depended on it. They had believed in the promise of fair treatment under the law. They had gone through the court system, ultimately relying on the constitutional checks and balances against arbitrary actions by the executive branch.

With the decision of the highest court in the United States behind them, they thought Native American nations would truly be able to live as allies of the Americans in peace and cooperation. But it was not to be. In one of the darkest episodes in American history, Jackson, despite his oath of office to protect and defend the Constitution, ignored the decision of the Supreme Court and stepped into the role of a military dictator. In effect, he nullified the Constitution. With no legal authority he unilaterally decided to settle "the Indian problem" in his own way, by force. While many people today have never heard of *Worcester vs. Georgia*, and are unaware that one of their presidents violated the Constitution by refusing to enforce a Supreme Court decision, saying, in effect, "the Chief Justice has made his decision, now let him enforce it," they have heard of its aftermath, The Trail of Tears.[10]

The Choctaws were the first to go. Under the terms of the Treaty of Dancing Rabbit Creek in 1831, they were herded off their land by the American military and made to walk on a death march through the Ozark Mountains to land outside the jurisdiction of the United States, the refugee lands that came to be called Oklahoma Territory.[11] Oklahoma is a single word made up of two Choctaw words, *okla*, which means people, and *humma*, which means red. Essentially, my ancestors knew that they were going to a place that would soon be populated by other Native American refugees. Therefore, they named it as a sanctuary for all "red people." It was also a sanctuary for all "red Christians." The Choctaws who died on the Trail of Tears were Christians.

The image of Christians driving other Christians off their land is not what most people associate with "how the West was won." Popular American history tends to portray the conflict between Native American nations and Western settlers in a much later time frame, well into the last decade of the nineteenth century when remnants of free Native peoples fought their last desperate campaigns against insurmountable odds. That image is accurate, but actually, not normative. The experience of the majority of the Native American population had nothing to do with covered wagons or warriors on horseback. It was far less dramatic, but just as deadly to Native rights. It occurred largely on paper, using intimidation more than cavalry charges.

Like the Godfather, the United States made Native people an offer they could not refuse. Under duress, they were made to sign treaties ceding huge portions of their land to the Federal government. These treaties were repeatedly broken by the American government as more land was confiscated and the people evicted by force. Native communities, usually already decimated by diseases for which they had no immunity, were stripped of their lands by fraudulent means, and then deported, either to concentration camps called reservations or to Oklahoma Territory. The majority of these people, the Native American survivors of ethnic cleansing, were Christians. Among the first buildings to be erected in the refugee centers of Oklahoma were churches. My great-grandfather was a Presbyterian pastor who is responsible for building several of these churches in Oklahoma. For many years around small communities like Ada and Marlow, they were simply called "the Charleston church." In the churches dotted across southeastern Oklahoma, Choctaws who survived the long walk into exile gathered to pray. They asked God to help them understand what had happened to them. They lifted up their lament to Jesus to help them in their affliction. They sang Choctaw hymns imagining a better day, a day of justice and redemption.

Christians cheating and oppressing Christians is the historic sub-text of most of the story between Native Americans and white people during the nineteenth century. Many of the appeals made by Native people in the courts or in the press during these decades include a call for justice in the name of God. Native American meetings called to rally efforts to hold off removal on the Trail of Tears included invocations to God for help and protection in the name of Jesus. As people were forced to walk into exile on the Trail of Tears they sang hymns and prayed for deliverance. As thousands, especially the smallest children and the elders, died from exposure on the death march they were buried in Christian services, their graves marked by crosses.

The Trail of Tears, therefore, brings us full circle to the grave-yard. Before the coming of Christianity, Choctaws buried their dead in communal graves. After conversion to Christianity, they buried them individually. The transition from one practice to another marks the path into the Wilderness for my people. The vision of my ancestors changed. Their quest changed. They went from an independent, prosperous, and thriving nation into a culturally shattered community of refugees. They lost the image of themselves as a chosen people of God, dwelling on sacred land in covenant with God. They saw them-selves instead as survivors of a cultural genocide in desperate need of a Messiah. Their quest altered from a search for personal meaning as members of a vital society into a search for legal strategies that could save them in the eleventh hour of their history from the greed and corruption of an oppressor's power. The spiritual aspect of their lives became a kind of vision quest because it became a lament. On the Trail of Tears, my ancestors were, quite literally, crying for a vision. They were being tested, driven out, sent into an unknown land as exiles by the waters of Babylon, longing for a sign from God in which they could hope.

What does this shared experience among the Choctaw, Cherokee, Creek, and Chickasaw people have to tell us about the first vision quest of Jesus? How does the gospel story in Matthew read when seen through the eyes of those Christians who are the survivors of this horrendous chapter in American history? The graveyard is a good place to begin looking for answers because how people treat the dead has a lot to tell us about how they treat the living. Prior to the arrival of Europeans, my ancestors had a very ritualized practice of preparing the dead for transition into the afterlife. In fact, one of the aspects of Christianity that was easy for Choctaws to adapt was the concept of everlasting life because the afterlife was conceived as being an extension of the everyday world we already know. Like the people of ancient Egypt, Native Americans traditionally thought there could be no more wonderful world than the one they had been gifted with by the Creator. Consequently, "heaven" was visualized as being very similar to Earth. It was a land of plenty, a place where people would continue doing what they ordinarily did in traditional Native religion: worship God in everything they did on a daily basis.

This theology of the afterlife underscores one of the hallmarks of Native America's original covenant. In traditional Native life, religion was a daily experience. Native people woke in prayer, went through their daily routine in a sacred manner, and ended the day in prayer. Life was religion. There were special ceremonies, of course, and unique moments like birth and death, but these were all woven into the fabric of an everyday spiritual life. There was no special day set aside to do "church." All days were equally precious, equally holy. This everyday sense of the sacred, which is what Native people believe will continue after death, means that the holy is accessible to everyone, everywhere, at every time. In traditional Native societies people could seek God in their own quest. They could interpret the meaning they believed God had for them. Their occupations as human beings were sanctified, whether they were hunters or homemakers, because the pattern of everyday life is exactly what God had designed for them from the very beginning. So there was not a great sense of hierarchy in most of the traditional Native American nations before 1492.

This is not to say that there were not Native nations with a sense of religious hierarchy. There were some, such as the one that developed into a great city state known as Cahokia.[12] But in general, the religious worldview that had evolved throughout North America was far more egalitarian, far more focused on a rhythm of everyday piety and special communal ceremonies. There might be spiritual specialists, the medicine people, who would either be consulted or who would preside over special events, but their role did not set them apart from the community at large. The whole of the nation was one great spiritual family and every member of that family had a direct channel to God through prayer and vision quest.

This explains why Choctaws gathered up the bones of their loved ones and placed them in little houses in the community before burying them in a mass grave. The burial practice mirrored the sacred way to live. As in life, so in death: each person would continue to live in the afterlife in the same sacred way they lived on earth; they would continue to be part of the people, of the sacred nation; they would live in community with God in heaven just as we live with God here in this mortal reality. The key theological principle at work is continuity, an unbroken thread of life that passes through death binding the community together in a bond undiminished by time.

Choctaws died as they lived: together. Because each Choctaw was one of the chosen people, because each Choctaw was equal in the eyes of God, because each Choctaw had a unique piece of the vision given to humanity by God, then each Choctaw was an intimate and integral part of the whole. Choctaws, like almost every other Native nation in North America maintained a cardinal spiritual understanding: life is not about the individual, life is about the community.

Andrew Jackson and his cronies did not share this spiritual vision with their Native American brothers and sisters who were Christian. Jackson prided himself as a rugged individualist. He was esteemed by other macho patriots of his age who also believed they were rugged individualists. Together, they saw their acts of fraud and intimidation against other Christians as their God given right to take what they wanted. They had the power. They had a plan. They were determined to erase Native Americans from the United States and let God sort out the survivors.

One of the most important distinctions between traditional Native American societies and European societies is this difference between individuality and individualism. Native Americans embrace individuality, but abhor individualism. In traditional Native communities people prized their own unique sense of who they were as individuals. In the vision quest, they often left on their quest with one name, but returned with another. Because of what they had seen or heard, they had been transformed. Therefore, to honor and celebrate this spiritual moment of transition, of growth and change, they would be given a new name by which the community recognized them. Echoes of this exist in European Christian tradition. When a person enters a religious order as a monk or nun he or she may have their name changed in order to signify this highlight of their spiritual evolution. What could be more individual then a personal name? And what could call more attention to a person than changing a name? Generations of European women with maiden names can attest to this kind of historic practice. Native Americans embraced their individuality in this and a variety of other ways.

I used to tell my seminary students to imagine driving through a suburban neighborhood and seeing every house painted with the dreams and visions of their occupants. That image allows us some idea of what it was like in Native cultures before the conquest of the Americas. People had a strong sense of their personal gifts and valued an appropriate sense of pride in each human being. The only restriction on pride was when it turned individuality into individualism, into *hubris*. That ancient Greek term, meaning overwhelming arrogance, is how traditional Native societies viewed the rugged individualism of people such as Andrew Jackson.

From the Native spiritual perspective, when a person loses their priority for living in community then they have broken the most sacred bond set down by God at the time of creation. The interrelatedness of all things, the kinship of humanity, and the sacredness of each person as a vital part of the whole are the foundational values of God's original covenant with Native America that must never be violated. Traditional Native America is built on the "we," not on the "I." God is the only singular. All of the rest of creation is plural. Human beings are never exceptions to this rule. Our humanity depends on it because while we may change our names to celebrate our spiritual journey, we never change our identity.

We are one of the tribe of the human beings. We are part of the People. We are inseparable from our family, our clan, our nation. This explains why the one punishment Native people feared the most for any egregious misdoing was not death by execution, but exile. Losing the "we" to only become an "I" was worse than death. It meant becoming a non-human. It was to be consigned to an eternal limbo from which there was no escape in either life or death.

Choctaws were buried together. They were individuals, but they never lost their identity as part of the People. Even under the persecution of the Trail of Tears, they kept traditional values alive in their Christian faith. They remembered Exodus 13:19: "Moses took the bones of Joseph with him because Joseph had made the Israelites swear an oath. He had said, 'God will surely come to your aid, and then you must carry my bones up from this place.'"

On the Trail of Tears some of the refugees carried the bones of their dead with them as best they could. They did not want to break the bond of family. They did not want to leave their loved ones behind. Others, who died along the way, had to be hurriedly buried on the road, their individual graves marked only by a rough cross. The resulting emotional trauma for my ancestors is almost beyond language to describe. Walking away from the ancient communal graves of generations of the People, desperately trying to bring some of them like the bones of Joseph on the journey ahead, having to inter elders and children alone, knowing they would never be found again, lost in a kind of limbo: the pain and suffering of the Choctaws and all of the Native peoples forced onto the Trail of Tears is worthy of a lament for all time.

It is a lament shared by Jesus, the Choctaw Messiah. In his first vision quest, according to Matthew (4:1–11), Jesus was "led by the Spirit into the desert to be tempted by the devil." Like the Choctaw people, he was going out into a wild place, a place unknown and potentially hostile. In keeping with the classic form of the vision quest, Jesus was entering a "lonely" place, a place set apart. He was being attended by an elder, the Spirit, who took him to a place to make his vision quest just as Few Tails had taken Black Elk. As the Native Messiah, Jesus was ready for this experience. He had prepared himself as custom had dictated. He had been cleansed, purified, by the waters of the Jordan River when his brother John baptized him. This fact alone has significance for Native people because, as we saw in the previous chapter, in the concept of family understood by many Native American nations John could be thought of as the brother of Jesus.

To understand the first vision quest of Jesus, it is critical to understand the nature of family. Traditional Native American families are not "nuclear." They are a matrix of relationships that encompass a wide spectrum of people. The children of siblings are not thought of as "nieces" or "nephews," but a person's own children.[13] These children would refer to what European culture characterizes as "uncles" or "aunts" with terms like "daddy" and "mommy." An "immediate" family, therefore, is made up of a number of people not included in European definitions.

In an even broader sense, these family members are gathered into the person's clan. The clan system is as central to Native culture as it is, for example, to Scottish culture. Clans are family. They establish kinship ties that are of paramount importance to traditional cultures. Among traditional Choctaws, for example, clans follow a matrilineal line. Many families are part of a specific clan and the people within the clan are understood to be so closely related that they cannot intermarry. Marriage can only take place outside the clan.[14]

As the Native Messiah, Jesus is a person with a deep sense of relatedness to a whole village of human beings who are direct members of his personal family. He carries a clan marker in his heart, an understanding of the intimate bond he shares with hundreds of other men, women, and children. He is their "brother," blood bonded to them. He is the "father" of children, probably of many children, since his own biological siblings and "cousin-siblings" would be married and parents of children. In the Native Covenant, it would be possible for these youngsters to call Jesus "Daddy," just as elsewhere in the gospel story Jesus refers to God as "Abba," Daddy.

As a brother and parent, as a member of his clan, Jesus goes out on his first vision quest representing the whole of his People. He knows that they are a nation because of their covenant with God. They call themselves the People, the tribe of the human beings, to announce this covenantal identity. Like Jesus, each member of the nation understands that he or she is a chosen person, living in community not by accident of birth or economic necessity, but by divine intention.

The individual Native person, therefore, carries a strong sense of being a child of God in covenant connection to all of the others in the nation. Jesus, as a "Son of the People," walks behind the Spirit into the Wilderness, not as a single mystic going out for a private audience with God, but as the representative of the whole nation going out to speak to their parent God. It is crucial to remember these many layers of relationship in the Native tradition embodied by Jesus in order to fully appreciate the impact of what God shows him.

As in the classic Native American vision quest, Jesus endures his quest while fasting. He does not take food or water. In this way, he cuts himself off from even the elemental connections he has to sustain himself in order to concentrate on what he must do to sustain others. In the Native vision quest, the focus is on what the individual must do to be part of the relational matrix of community. Therefore, when Jesus receives his first vision, it is not surprising that it comes from the oldest members of this community: the stones of the Earth. In the traditional Native spiritual understanding, all of creation is endowed with the spirit of God. The very fact that God imagined something into being means that that object of creation has the mind of God within it. The nature of God, the essence of God, the love of God have touched all things, for nothing exists that is outside of God.

For this reason, many Native traditions speak of the stones of the Earth as our oldest relatives in a spiritual sense. Stones have known the mind of God for a very long time, from a time before time. Therefore, Native people pay attention to stones, to rocks and mountains and canyons because these first elements embody the ancient will of God in creation. The intention of God in creating the Earth is so powerful, so extraordinarily holy, that the echo of that divine love remains present even after uncounted centuries have passed. As the Native Messiah, Jesus stands in his sacred circle, not only looking up to the sky, but down to the Earth. He pays attention to the stones around him in the desert. And in his hunger, he imagines them as loaves of bread on the desert floor. What did the stones have to teach him? Are they physical nourishment for him alone or spiritual nourishment of a different kind? In the Native Covenant they are the oldest "living" things. A theological principle is embodied in them: a single stone, a single God. The stones would have reminded Jesus of this truth. In effect, they would have been expressing the same monotheistic formula found in ancient Israel, God is One.

This is why traditional Native American medicine bundles, the personal collection of sacred objects kept by Native people to remind them of their vision quests, contain stones. Human beings cannot make stones. They cannot create as God creates. Only God, the maker of all things, has that power. The stones of the Earth, from the Native Covenant perspective, are present in a vision quest as a foundational affirmation of the singularity and unity of God. They are literally the rock on which the Native Covenant is built. By affirming the power of the one true God, they caution us not to fall into the temptation of thinking too highly of ourselves.

The monotheistic parallel between the Native and Hebrew Covenants is apparent in the first vision quest of Jesus, but there are significant differences in how the two religious cultures would interpret the Temptation. A key figure in this first vision quest is the personification of evil in the form of a Devil. I think it is important to acknowledge that Native tradition would not have an equivalent personality in its theology. There could be evil spirits or evil people, but there would not have been this unique character of a fallen angel who is the global mastermind of evil. In a more traditional Native interpretation, the personification of evil in the form of a "Devil" is more accurately characterized in the projection of "Self."

In the Native Covenant the devil is within. Native tradition does not need to create a single universal figure of evil because the true universal nature of evil is that it is within all of us. The temptation to rugged individualism is always present. It is the trap of "self," the temptation to put one's own needs over the needs of the community. It is fitting that the stones confront Jesus with this mirror into his own sense of self because ego is one of the most primal of all spiritual mistakes. From the Native American viewpoint, the lure of personal desire is the core of destruction. Native tradition is very similar to Buddhism in this regard. Both traditions identify the unmitigated sense of self as a pathway to deep spiritual error.

Jesus, as the Native Messiah, understands what his oldest relatives, the stones, are trying to tell him. They are the many that embody the One. They are not there just for him, but for the People. In recognizing that truth, Jesus understands how his own mind is putting him to the test. His profession of faith – "the People do not live by bread alone but by every word that comes from the mouth of God"[15] – would be the way that the stones helped him to return to proper spiritual balance. The vision of the stones establishes from the outset of his quest that he will be true to the oldest principle of the Native Covenant. He will stay grounded in the faith in the One God. He will not let any sense of self lure him away from his calling to be one with the People. Spiritual unity will be maintained, and therefore, spiritual equilibrium. The many will always be the one.

The second vision of his first quest is a sky vision. Like many traditional Native vision quests, the Native Messiah would have chosen a "high and holy place." Often the traditional vision quest took place on a mountain, a hill or a butte. These were places with a view. They would allow the person making the quest to see the world around them. When I made my own first quest, I chose to go to the roof of my apartment building, not to the basement. I instinctively wanted to be in the open. I wanted to see out. I wanted to be in a place where I could also be seen by God. What was the meaning of the sky vision for Jesus? What did he see when he looked out to the world around him?

One of the ironies of the vision quest is that the person stands on a tiny circle of land, but that circle encompasses the whole universe. In his first vision quest in the wilderness, Jesus looks out at the endless sky, the metaphor for forever. Poised on this spiritual edge, the connecting point between his own finite circle of reality and the limitless expanse of God's reality, Jesus hangs on the brink of faith. Matthew's text says that the Devil, that voice that Native tradition identifies as the Self, tempts him to "throw himself down" from his high place so he will force God to save him.

The idea that Jesus is tempted to test God is one that Native Christians can certainly understand, but our reading of this vision has a slightly different nuance. The image of the Native Messiah teetering between God and God's creation, between the earth and the sky, raises theological imagery from the Native Covenant about the harmonious relationship between Mother Earth, the tribe of the human beings, and the Maker of All Things. The "test" implied in this vision is not only about the Messiah's right relationship with God (and, therefore, humanity's relationship to God), but also on the other end of the alignment, about the relationship to Mother Earth.

Any human ego is capable of imagining "the sky is the limit." We can be tempted to imagine that everything out there is up for grabs. We can become covetous, greedy, desiring to possess whatever we see. Sitting on a small patch of real estate, we may begin to think that there should be more. In fact, that we deserve more. The open sky, the endless expanse of creation, becomes not an object of wonder, but an object of plunder. One of the most bizarre things about European colonizers from the Native American perspective was their insane idea that they could "own the earth." Traditional Native American societies do not have a concept of land ownership. The land is granted by God to the People in sacred trust as part of the Native Covenant. It is, and remains, the creation of God. Human beings are the stewards of the land, caretakers only and not owners. They are responsible for maintaining it, sharing it, and enjoying it. Therefore, looking out to the world, they see a garden of blessing.

European colonists saw profit. They saw an endless resource that could be conquered, claimed, owned, used. The spiritual vision of the invaders was both incredibly narrow (every little piece of property had to belong to them) and incredibly broad (they never stopped wanting more). The vision of the sky illustrates this fundamental temptation for the Native Messiah. Is the right relationship to all that there is a question of stewardship or of ownership? Which will it be?

The profession of faith by the Native Messiah sends a resounding answer in affirmation of the Native Covenant. The Earth is a living being. She is personified in female imagery to underscore her role as the source of life. Earth, therefore, is Mother because the vast network of life, the systems of life, of which human beings are only a small part, is sacred. God designs them for a divine purpose. They maintain the universal balance of relationships ordained by God from the beginning of creation.

For human beings to break that chain of kinship (for us to throw ourselves down to test it) would be a spiritual disaster. We are not to insult God by claiming that we can use the creation for our own purposes, much less for profit. We are not the masters of all we see. We cannot swallow the universe into the stomach of our own greed. We do not need more. The ethic implicit in a culture that understands family as a vast matrix of kinship is an ethic of sharing. The sky vision shows Jesus the fundamental value of Native life: it is to be lived in a spirit of stewardship. Human beings are entrusted with everything they see. They are responsible for it. They are to be in awe of it. They are to delight in it.

As the Native Messiah, Jesus faces the vision of the sky as a choice. Greed is always a possibility. The self can lead any person to become jealous, to be envious, to want more. Control is always an option. Native Americans are not any more immune to these temptations than anyone else. It is a part of human nature; even the most spiritual steward can become jealous of the true owner. In his sky vision Jesus announces what the Native Covenant would say: "do not put God to the test."[16] In other words, do not imagine that you can stand in the place of God by claiming title to creation. The presumption of such a claim is an affront to the very nature of creation itself. It violates every bond of family, clan, and community that holds not only the People, but all creation in balance and harmony.

If you allow self to tip those scales of pride, if you permit individuals to imagine that they can actually own and use creation just
for themselves, then you have denied God. It is that simple. The
person who stands in even the smallest circle of land and looks out
to the vast expanse of the universe with awe and respect receives it
all as a blessing from God, a promise of life that will be kept forever by the sacred covenant between God and the People. However,
the person who imagines they must always have more loses even the
smallest part of the promise, consigning themselves and their People
into a rapacious hunger that consumes the Earth, until they wither
into dust, only to be blown away into an empty sky.

The last vision Jesus receives on his first quest is the vision of a
mountain. In Native tradition, mountains are sacred places. Among
the Navajo, for example, there are four holy mountains that mark the
boundaries of their world. Among the Lakota, the Black Hills are especially sacred. The Native American novelist, N. Scott Momaday, wrote
a novel called *The Way To Rainy Mountain*, about the sacred mountain of his Kiowa people. Even among those of us who come from
lowlands like my Choctaw ancestors, there are sacred "mountains,"
places like *Nanih Waiya*, the holy mounds that still dot the countryside
throughout the Mississippi River region from Canada to the Gulf.[17]

Mountains are sites of spiritual power in Native tradition. They are
signposts to the presence of God. They are meeting grounds for the
spirits of both ancestors and animals that reside unseen, but never
unfelt, in the holy landscape of Native tradition. Therefore, when
Jesus imagines that he is going up a mountain, he is ascending in a
spiritual way to receive the final vision of his first quest. Because it
comes to him on a mountain, it comes from the combined power of
all that is alive in the spiritual realm. Mountains are spirit-filled. They
are like a camp meeting for what European Christians would call "the
great cloud of witness," the place where these clouds of spirit seem
to be caught, mingled, and held into place by the anchor of the great
mountain. It is no wonder to Native Christians that Moses went up
Sinai to receive his vision of the tablets. In the same way, Jesus would
go up the mountain to understand his role in life as a spiritual person.

The purpose of the vision quest in Native tradition is to reveal how a person is to live in a spiritual way to help his or her people. The quest can show us what our holy assignment is to be, what gifts we have to share, or what work we can accomplish in bringing good medicine home with us. Among all of these possibilities, only one is missing: we never receive a vision that shows us how to be above others.

People who place the bones of their dead together in a common grave do not believe that some people have a right to be buried in grand mausoleums. The pharaohs of Egypt wanted their burial sites to be unmistakably huge and imposing; the Emperors of China wanted armies of terracotta soldiers to guard them in their final resting place; the great leaders of the West are still interred in graves that seek to set them apart as special beings. The vision of the mountain would say to Native Christians, "It shall not be so among you."[18]

In the Dakotas I would have to ask friends to point out the medicine man or medicine woman for me when we were at a gathering. You could not spot them. They wore no special clothing, no signs of office, no hints of who they were other than a part of the community. To catch the cultural nuance, imagine the Pope dressed like any other person on the street.

The vision of the mountain took Jesus to the heights of spiritual power and surrounded him with the presence of the spirits, a cloud of witnesses. The temptation of the self to imagine that he is, therefore, better than others confronts him, just as it confronts any of us who inflate ourselves with power or status. In response, the Native Messiah asserts that he is only one of the People. Jesus calls out from the mountaintop: "worship only God and serve God alone."[19] He proclaims that in a community sealed under the Native Covenant there are no hierarchies. There are many roles to be filled, many visions to be shared, and some of us may be granted an especially powerful vision, but in the end we are all only servants of God, only one small part of a much greater mountain.

Native Christian theology offers us a radical sense of community. The vision of the mountain reminds Jesus that just as no one can be on "top," no one can be on the "bottom" either. In his vision there is no vertical caste system for human beings. Though we may have very different gifts and very different abilities, we are all members of a single sacred family that stretches out horizontally to incorporate all persons without exception. We are a spirit family. We include our ancestors. We include clans of creatures whose presence on Earth is just as important as our own. Only God stands apart. The Creator is at the center of all life, the One being around whom we all revolve in an attitude of joy and thanksgiving.

When the Native Messiah completed his first vision quest, he returned to be greeted by his friends. In this case, his spirit friends. Matthew's narrative calls these beings "angels." Native tradition would call them "spirits." They are at the end of the story to symbolize that the person on the quest goes out from community and always returns to community. There is no real break in the relationship with the tribe of the human beings.

Matthew, therefore, offers a description of the first vision quest of Jesus that can be read as an expression of the most fundamental values and teachings in the Native Covenant. This vision quest announces the Good Medicine of Jesus as being deeply grounded in Native American religious tradition. Jesus embodies a Native concept of messiahship because he confirms the cardinal principles of Native tradition. In his vision, he supports the primacy of God, the centrality of the "we" over the "I," the egalitarian nature of sacred community. Jesus rejects the rugged individualism that inflates the human ego and leads to the exploitation of greed. He stands against those temptations that are truly devilish in every human heart, the lure of ego and profit.

As the Native Messiah, Jesus embodies every virtue of the Native tradition while preparing himself to contest those forces that may try to subvert the People. He returns from his wilderness experience even more connected to the Native family. His vision is so powerful that he cannot be seen in the crowd. He is truly one with the many.

When my ancestors buried their loved ones in a common grave, when they carried their bones on the long walk into the wilderness, they were on a vision quest with Jesus. They were announcing that what holds us together as human beings, what unites us to all of God's holy creation, must be the primary vision of our collective lives. My Choctaw relatives, along with those of so many other Native nations, were making their witness to God. Even during the nightmare and trauma of Removal, of the Trail of Tears, they kept their vision clear. They walked with Jesus, the Native Messiah on the path of stones, under the open sky, toward the next sacred mountain. They did not waver in their trust in the one great human family, the origin and the destination of all that we are and all that we were ever meant to be.

Chapter 7

THE MOUNTAIN

In 1680 the several small communities known as the Pueblo people of the southwestern part of North America rose up in revolt against their Spanish occupiers. Among them were the farmers known as the Hopi, a name that translates into English as the "Peaceful Ones."[1] These men and women, renowned for their religion of peaceful coexistence, attacked and killed every Spanish settler they could find, including every priest and friar of the Catholic Church. Once the killing was done, they dismantled the Catholic mission, tearing it down stone by stone, scattering the evidence of the church until it was no longer visible. To put their actions into context, imagine the Amish suddenly going on a killing spree, massacring every Catholic they could find and tearing down their churches so that not even the foundations remained. What could have provoked the peaceful Hopi into such an act of desperate vengeance? For centuries, these quiet people had remained pacifists, preferring to move rather than fight, living on isolated mesa tops in the desert in order to avoid conflicts with any neighbors. What had caused them to change? What had driven them to set aside their deepest spiritual beliefs? What had caused them to murder other human beings? Searching for answers brings us to the heart of the second vision quest of Jesus.

Like every Native nation, the story of the Hopi begins in mystery. The Hopi themselves trace their beginnings to the Hisatsinom, their ancestors who built the beautiful cliff dwellings that still nestle in canyon walls throughout the Four Corners region of the American southwest where Arizona, New Mexico, Colorado and Utah meet.[2]

For some seven hundred years, from around 600 to 1300 CE, these early Hopi people built apartment-like structures and underground worship sites called *kivas* beneath the natural overhanging cliffs of the canyons. However, according to Hopi religion, even these ancient places were only part of a much longer narrative of migration going back to the dawn of human history, to what the Hopi call the Emergence, when human life first came out of the Earth to populate the world according to the will of God.

The mystery remains. Archeology suggests that the Hopi may have once lived on the desert plateaus before descending into the canyons, but where they came from before that is unknown. As with all Native peoples in North America, the thread of historical fact frays at the end of a brief timespan, leaving only the spiritual memory of the People to recollect early migrations across the continent. For the Hopi, this memory is especially vivid and important. Hopi religion is based on a cosmology that rivals that of Hinduism. Their sense of origins goes back to a layered theology of the successive creation and destruction of life on Earth, a kind of religious echo of the paleontological record of mass extinctions and rebirths.

For the Hopi, we are living in the Fourth World. Each of the earlier worlds was created by the thought of God, a distinction Hopi would make from Christians and Jews who describe genesis as an act of the Word. Hopi theology takes the act of creation back one more step into the mind of God, asserting that even before the Word there must be the Thought.

Like Hinduism, Hopi tradition places the locus of existence in the mind of the Creator and from that source emerges a vast and intricate succession of evolutions, pantheons, and relationships. The natural world and its human inhabitants are understood to have existed in different epochs, each rising and falling through time, until the current incarnation of life was reached. As this Fourth World began, human beings came out from the womb of the Earth, emerging into the daylight, being nurtured by supernatural benefactors: the spirits and the natural allies of both the plant and animal realm. Once human beings were born into the world in this way, coming out like infants into reality, they began their epic migrations.

Like ancient Israel, they began a search for their promised land, guided by God and enduring many tests along the way, but always journeying to the place where they would establish their sacred home. After their long residence in the cliff dwellings, the Hopi resumed their search until they found the mesa tops of what is now northeastern Arizona. Here they established four original communities, among them the oldest continuously occupied place in North America, Oraibi, the village of the Third Mesa. From these high vantage points, the Hopi lived in peace, farming the land below generation after generation, practicing their ancient traditions in the underground *kivas* that are as characteristic of their faith as cathedrals are to Christianity.

Many years ago, when I was making my vision quest on the rooftop in Cambridge, Massachusetts, I was asked to record a series of morning devotions for a local television station. This was in the day of the "sunrise sermon" on TV, a five-minute opening devotion that started the broadcast day at 5:00 am. I remember thinking that I might be the only person to ever see what I created, but I made a week's worth of five-minute spots, each one talking about Native American religion.

To be honest, I have forgotten all of the spots I made except for one. I still remember the spot I recorded talking about Hopi tradition. I explained that kivas were Hopi ceremonial sites, circular underground chambers accessed from an enclosed roof by a single ladder. I said that they were metaphors for the womb of the Earth from which humanity had emerged at the time of the Fourth World. I tried to capture the essence of how these *kivas* were used, what they ultimately meant for the Hopi People, by saying: "you have to imagine that these *kivas* are the spiritual control centers for spaceship Earth. What goes on in them guides our whole planet through time and space. Without the careful work of the Hopi at the controls we would crash and burn." Now, over forty years later, I cannot think of a better way to say it. The subtlety and the sophistication of the *kiva* tradition is exactly that: a complex array of sacred controls all linked to the matrix of existence that are maintained and operated by Hopi spiritual practitioners in order to preserve, protect, and nurture life in this dimension for the sake of all living things.

Hopi are the "peaceful people," not only from an ethic of nonviolence, but from a deep core theology of being life-givers to all reality. They are the mothers of life, the midwives of birth, the nurses of creation. The Hopi go down into their *kivas* and dance on their pueblo plazas in order to carry out their sacred calling. For longer than they can remember they have been taking care of us all. They have held creation in their care, feeling responsible not only for other humans, but for every living thing. Therefore, for the Hopi to wantonly take life is as unimaginable as for the Dalai Lama to be unmasked as a serial killer. It just does not compute. What happened?

Francisco Vasquez de Coronado happened. In 1540 his expedition to discover lost cities of gold brought him into Hopi territory. One of his lieutenants, Don Pedro de Tovar, made contact with the Hopi at the village of Awatovi. From that fateful encounter the rest of Hopi history turned slowly, but inexorably toward sorrow. The Spanish did not colonize Hopi lands right away; there was not much there for them to plunder. The Hopi were corn farmers with no great store of gold or silver to tempt the Europeans. For many years, therefore, the Spanish were aware of the Hopi, but not concerned with them. However, by 1629 the colonizers decided it was time to convert the Hopi (along with other Pueblo nations) to the Christian faith. They established a mission at Awatovi and sent some thirty friars to fan out and begin dismantling the traditional Native religion. Among the Hopi, this proved to be very difficult. Their tradition was so integral to their culture that abandoning it was tantamount to cultural suicide. More than that, for the Hopi to cease performing their annual rituals to maintain life was tantamount to cosmic suicide. They would be responsible for nothing less than the destruction of all life on our planet.

The Catholic friars found few converts. Hopi villages respected Christianity as the religion of the Spaniards, but vehemently resisted it as an option for them, especially if it meant leaving their sacred work at the controls of life in the *kiva*. Instead, they called on their partners in this holy mission to stand by them and protect them from Christian conversion. These partners were the Hopi's celestial reinforcements, the *katsinas*.[3]

The *katsinas* are Spirits, the embodiment of life in all of its forms, the powerful partners of the Hopi in maintaining balance and harmony on the planet. Again, the Hindu parallel is helpful. Just as Hinduism understands a single creator, but a pantheon of gods embodying different aspects of creation, so do the Hopis recognize God as the single source to life, but they honor many different Spirits as manifestations of God's sacred order. Hopi actively work with them to perform their task of preserving life. There are *katsinas* for natural wonders like the sun and stars, for other creatures like birds and insects, and for plant life like corn and flowers. Each one is represented with a distinctive form, like the statues of Christian saints, adorned with special clothing and colors to signify their sacred role in God's creation. Hopi dancers can put on costumes to embody these Spirits, signifying that they are sacramentally present in Hopi worship, an outward and visible sign of the inward, unseen reality of the Spirits coming into the human experience to lend support and spiritual power to the moment.

When the Catholic priests demanded that the Hopi burn the images of the *katsinas*, they were asking for an act of complete sacrilege. To break the relationship with the *katsinas* would be to sever humanity's ties to all other forms of life. It would mean that the moon would no longer bring the tides, the bees would no longer pollinate the flowers, and the corn would no longer grow to feed the people. Hopi people existed in a sophisticated vision of the natural cycles of life. They understood a scientific interrelationship between the different agencies and aspects of life. Until well into the nineteenth century the Hopi's worldview was far more akin to our current image of the Earth as an integrated life system than that of the European colonizers. The *katsinas* were not idols. They were not the simplistic images of a pagan culture that could not grasp the "higher" theology of the church. Rather, they were symbolic of both a rational and spiritual matrix of enormous complexity and coherence. For the Hopi, what the friars were offering seemed like simplistic superstition.

Consequently, the Hopi resisted conversion. They did so peacefully and politely, in keeping with the nonviolent style of life known as the Hopi Way. Actually, they predated their Hindu counterparts in practicing *Satyagraha*, the word for non-violent "non-cooperation" advocated by Gandhi hundreds of years later with his people's European colonizers. Unfortunately, the seventeenth century Spanish were not as restrained as the twentieth century British.

Faced with the refusal of the Hopi to deny their faith and adopt Roman Catholicism, the Spanish began a policy of brutal reprisals against the Peaceful Ones. They enslaved the Hopi, demanding hard labor and total obedience. They confiscated Hopi crops and left the people only survival subsistence. They forced the Hopi to build more churches and they forbid the practice of Hopi ceremonies. Hopi were literally beaten into submission, denied their religion and their dignity. It is a testimony to the sheer depth of faith among the Hopi in their traditional faith that they endured this misery for years. The cruelty was unrelenting, but the Hopi accepted it, continuing to resist conversion and carrying out their ceremonies in secret. From 1629 to 1680, the long suffering of the Hopi people continued until finally even their peaceful willpower snapped and violence swept through the Pueblos. It is called the Pueblo Revolt, a major turning point in not only Hopi history, but in the history of all North American Native nations.[4] For one thing, the Pueblo Revolt gave Native Americans something they had never had in millennia of their cultural evolution on this continent: a domesticated animal larger than a dog.

What many people do not realize is that Native Americans walked across their world. They did not ride because there was nothing to ride. The last forms of the horse or camel had gone extinct in North America long before domestication. Only the llama and the alpaca remained in the Andes as options for Native societies to use as pack animals. Otherwise, Native people walked wherever they went, carrying their burdens on their shoulders.

The horse was power. It was freedom. Which is exactly why the Spanish forbid any Native person from riding one. Horses were strictly reserved to the conquerors. They provided the extra leverage of control, of shock and awe, to keep the indigenous population pacified. But once the Pueblo Revolt occurred, once the masters of the horse were killed, the horses themselves became available to Native cultures. Within only a generation, the horse revolutionized Native life. Today, a great many people imagine the horse as synonymous with Native culture. They see Plains people on horseback, hunting the buffalo. But before 1680, the Plains nations were on foot and they hunted the buffalo from the ground, literally crawling close enough to pick them off or trying to drive them over cliffs. Only after the Pueblo people had sent horses out into the wild, making them available to other Native people to catch and tame, did Plains people become a horse culture.

The Revolt, therefore, was life changing for Native nations. It is celebrated as an act of liberation of epic proportions. After years of enslavement and brutality, the peaceful Pueblo communities rose up overnight, catching their oppressors completely off guard, attacking them with a ferocity fueled by memories of torture and degradation. The Spanish were all killed or chased away. So complete was the rout that they did not return for twenty years. In the meantime, the Hopi turned on the greatest symbol for their rage and resistance. They systematically dismembered the Christian churches stone by stone. They left no trace of what they saw as a threat to all life, a cult of death.

This incredible experience for the Hopi people offers us a startling and sobering vision of the real power of spiritual transfiguration. The metamorphosis of a community of farmers, a society as committed to nonviolence as the Amish, into a lightning strike of violent retribution, illustrates the forces that can overwhelm our control if we do not treat them with great care and respect. Under the pressure of dehumanization, the Hopi reacted. They transformed themselves. They turned inside out spiritually and became the antithesis of their own ideal. In a galvanizing moment, their religious vision went from one extreme to another, mutated by the chemistry of the human soul, which can endure heroically for the sake of a belief, but also strike out viciously for exactly the same reason.

As strange as it may seem, this undervalued part of Native American history has a great deal to tell us about the Christian gospel. At first glance, it would seem to be a total rejection of Christianity, a validation of all the horror stories of European colonialism and Christian imperialism. It would be easy to make the Hopi into the poster children for a campaign against Christian missionaries. However, if we go beneath the layers of racism and oppression to the spiritual center of the story, we begin to see a different vision: a vision of God and humanity that transcends the narrative of Spanish greed and Native courage. In fact, we come to a place we can only describe as a transfiguration.

In Matthew 17: 1–8 we are told a strange story, the second vision quest of Jesus. Like the first vision quest, this one has all of the classic elements of a traditional Native American quest. Jesus has prepared himself; his lament is so deep that he has predicted his own death. He goes up to a high place, accompanied by his spiritual supporters, his three disciples, Peter, James, and John. He stands alone before God. A vision occurs, but this time one so powerful that his friends actually see it. The vision includes a voice, one that is audible to the disciples of Jesus. The second vision quest of Jesus is a defining experience. But not only for Peter, James, and John. I believe it is akin to the spiritual experience of the Hopi people as well. It is a vision and a voice the Hopi people believe they also saw and heard long ago. It was a moment of their transfiguration too.

What made the Hopi cling so tenaciously to their religion? I believe it was because, at some point in their ancient migration, they saw something transcendent like Peter, James, and John saw. As the Hisatsinom, the Hopi ancestors walked on their long migration into the Fourth World. They emerged from darkness into light. They saw the spiritual power we describe as transfiguration. This vision was a cultural revelation, an insight, into the very nature of God. The moment was radiant. In their religious consciousness, the Hopi discerned the scientific, evolutionary nature of life. It was no longer just rocks and trees, birds and animals, people and spirits, but a vast interwoven network of relationships from the most minute to the most massive. For the Hopi, it was as if they could see into the mind of God. They could see how creation works.

The Hopi had an epiphany that would not come again until Western scientific theory began to peel back the layers of interrelatedness in the natural world. Europeans did it over centuries of study, using technology, but the Hopi did it with spiritual intuition over centuries of religious inquiry. In their migration they had watched the cycles of the seasons, the movement of the stars, the patterns of plant life, and the habits of the animals. With a gift for religious rationalism, they connected the dots. They began to construct the big picture of God's creation: a harmonious and finely balanced symphony of life forms, all interacting, all interdependent. In this revelation, the universe opened up to them. They saw how thought alone could be the origin for creation. They envisioned the Earth as a sphere and in their symbolism placed two twin brothers at the "top" and "bottom," mythic figures who helped to hold the planet in equilibrium. They went on to identify many of the major players in the process of existence, both animate and inanimate: the *katsinas* who were as much a part of the shared reality as human beings. And finally, they placed themselves, the Peaceful Ones, into this vision of wholeness and cooperation. They made themselves agents of evolution, stewards of environmental balance. It was a vision light years beyond what the Spanish friars could have comprehended. In Spain the church was actively persecuting scientists for making discoveries the Hopi had achieved generations before. The church was trying to stifle this kind of scientific vision. The *kiva* was embracing it.

What Peter, James, and John saw was a vision of Jesus transfigured, altered from an ordinary person into a being of celestial light. They glimpsed the raw power of the divine plan made present in human time and space. It was as if they were observing atomic fission up close. The Hopi vision was just as powerful; they realized what they were dealing with in their cosmic revelation was nothing more nor less than the power of life and death. Transfiguration can create, but it can also destroy. The true forces of Nature are sustaining to human life, but they are also potential threats to our existence. Rain can become floods. Wind can become tornadoes. The earth can shake. The animals can disappear. On their long migration into the desert canyons, the Hopi had witnessed all of these truths. They had seen drought. They had known hunger. They had watched the animals leave never to return. Their crops had failed. Therefore, they understood the finely tuned nature of the power with which they were dealing.

Their vision of Nature was dazzling, but it could become blinding. Careful attention had to be paid to keep the energies of creation in equilibrium. Ecological balance required effort. Environmental stewardship did not just take care of itself. Excesses or neglect, either one, could tip the scales and bring disaster. The Hopi theology centered on the delicate issues of monitoring the health of life by watching the dials on the power of life. The *kiva* truly was the command center, the place where Hopi spiritual technicians kept the power of their radiant vision in alignment.

Jesus appears in his second vision quest as the pure power of the divine come to Earth. He personifies transfiguration because he embodies the full force of God's creative energy in one place at one time. Like the Hopi spiritual understanding, he shows us that we are dealing with forces far beyond our control. The power of Jesus, the energy of God in the world, can work wonders, transforming life, but if we misunderstand it, if we seek to misuse it, it can bring disaster on us.

From a Native American reading of the second vision quest, the mistake of Peter is the mistake of the Spanish friars. They believed they could build a box to contain the power of God and use it for their own ends. They did not see the gleaming power of a world held in balance by the participation of all living things, a partnership with the forces of nature, the *katsinas* who are outside any human authority. Instead, they saw another chance to grab for power itself, to assert the dominance of one community over another. In so doing, they violated the spiritual protocols of harmony so important to the

Hopi religion and started a chain reaction leading to a meltdown, a kind of spiritual Chernobyl in the desert.

Peter wanted to build his booth in order to keep the vision contained. The Hopi understood the divine vision could never be pocketed by human beings. It could only be maintained within the spiritual stasis represented by Moses and Elijah. In their cosmology, the Hopi were very accustomed to the image of two poles that held energy in tension.

Part of their genius as religious scientists was the concept of two poles transmitting reciprocal energy: Poganghoya and Palongawhoya, the North and South poles. They are twin brothers. Between them stands all of the power of life on Earth. They are symbolic reminders of how that power must be cared for and respected. Moses and Elijah are the twin brothers of the second vision quest. They stand on either side of Jesus. They are symbolic of the tradition that must be maintained if the energy of the Transfiguration is to be appreciated and channeled into sustaining life. They represent the response to the vision that takes us beyond Peter's small-minded desire to limit it to any one religious container.

The Hopi died rather than give up the tradition of their elders, of their Hitsatsinom. Moses and Elijah, the embodiment of elders, do not stand outside the vision, but within it. They are integral to it. The Hopi did not cling to the past out of some misguided attachment to old superstitions, but rather as a fundamental theological principle. Tradition is the only true container for vision. Tradition is the bearer of revelation. Tradition is not a thing of the past, but of the future. The message of Jesus as the Native Messiah is balanced in the energy field of tradition. It is not to be received as separate from what our ancestors have experienced; it is not a disembodied new idea being handed to us by another culture; it is not in the box of any denomination or culture. The gospel of the Native Jesus is held within the embrace of Native American spiritual tradition. It is a power of transformation that serves the people and honors the teaching of the ancestors.

To receive it, the Native people only need to respect their own Covenant. Unlike what the Spanish conquerors tried to tell us, we do not have to deny ourselves and our own history. The second vision quest is a bright reminder that our future is our past made new. The ancient wisdom of the Hopi, as for all Native nations, is integral to the new Covenant of the Native Messiah. The two emerge from the same source. They are part of the same story. What the ancestors saw is what we see today, if we look through their eyes to behold the power of God in our lives. Ultimately, this is why the cloud of mystery descends over the mesa. The arrogant assumption of any one people that their experience alone contains the truth, the religious paranoia that demands total conformity to any one cultural expression of faith, is exposed as the opposite of true vision when the cloud descends.

One of the most common names for God among traditional Native American societies is the Great Mystery. This name was accorded to God because Native people understood that when all was said and done, the function of the vision quest was not to take away mystery, but rather, to lead us deeper into mystery. As bright as the vision may be, it resides in the mystery that is God; it resides in a cloud we can never penetrate.

The *kiva* is a place of mystery. It is a shadowy world within a world, deep and hidden from view. When the Hopi enter the *kiva*, they are entering a place of mystery. They are acknowledging that there is a power, a wisdom greater than our own intellect. As wise as our ancestors have been in putting together the intricate pieces of the puzzle we call life, they were still only stewards of the mystery of God. When the cloud comes down on the disciples, it does so to illustrate our spiritual blindness. The desire to keep God's vision for ourselves is short-sighted. Only when we give up the desire to control the power of God do we truly understand our role in creation.

The Hopi knew that human beings can make things better or we can make things worse. We can work with the *katsinas* or we can ignore them. We have free will and our choices matter. How we respect our traditions and attend to our rituals matters, but it does not elevate us above the Creator. We are the technicians of grace, not the source. We must always remember that we are living in this world, but there have been others in the past. There will be more in the future. This is our time, our moment of choice. The mystery of God is not ours to own, only to serve, which is why the Voice in the second vision quest of Jesus simply tells us to do what any good Hopi knows to do when it comes to God: be quiet and pay attention.

Through all their years of suffering, the Hopi remained quiet, but they paid attention. They kept their eye on the vision of the transfiguration entrusted to their ancestors. They continued to perform the vital ceremonies that kept life in balance. They never forgot the *katsinas* and they never lost hope in the future of humanity. At the end of his second vision quest, Jesus comes to his friends and tells them, "Get up. Don't be afraid." Those few words of strength are part of the vision because they represent what sustains human beings. The spirit of the Hopi could not be broken by the Spanish or in later years by other conquerors.

I wish I could write an end to this chapter by saying that the Hopi threw off the yoke of their oppression and lived forever as free people, but that is not the case. In 1700, the Spanish returned. They forced the Pueblo people back into submission and they returned to their efforts to convert the Hopi to Christianity. Once again, the Hopi resisted. Generation after generation, they held on to their beliefs. Perhaps, in their own way, they whispered to one another: "get up, don't be afraid." By 1849 the Spanish had been supplanted by the Americans. Protestant and Mormon missionaries joined the Catholics. Still the Hopi resisted. By 1875 a boarding school was built to teach Hopi children. It was designed to promote the doctrine of assimilation common to that era among white people who thought themselves enlightened. The school made the children wear white styles of clothing; it cut their hair and required them to speak only English; it instructed them in the Baptist theology of Christianity; it taught the boys to work with their hands and the girls to sew. The white founders of the school and their Christian supporters thought the school was a modern way to convert the Hopi, but the Hopi rejected the idea and few Hopi children attended the school.

In 1890 the frustrated Indian agents sent to administer Hopi life literally kidnapped Hopi children from their families and deported them to the school. There they suffered corporeal punishment if they did not assimilate to white standards, including conversion to Christianity. Nineteen Hopi parents who tried to protest and demand a return of their children were arrested and spent a year in the maximum security prison on Alcatraz Island.[5] The Federal Government wanted to demonstrate in no uncertain terms to the Hopi that their resistance was futile and that they would become both Christianized and Americanized no matter what.

The social and cultural disruption that these recent years of oppression brought to Hopi people is difficult to quantify. Families were torn apart. Villages fragmented. Individuals were thrown into despair and self-destructive behavior. And yet, miraculously, the old Hopi traditions survived. The attacks on them did not subside until well into the twentieth century, and in spite of all that any outside power could do, the Hopi held on to their traditions. They got up. They were not afraid. They kept their vision.

The Hopi experience illustrates the meaning of transfiguration. It shows us why the Native Messiah blesses and protects the Native Covenant. On the Mesa of the Transfiguration, the vast power of God was revealed to humankind. For one shining moment, we were allowed to glimpse into the mind that created the first thought of creation. The complexity of that thought, its intricacies and balances, were beyond the scope of human reason. All we can do, as Native American tradition tells us over and over, is to stand in awe of the creation and marvel at how it works together, every piece and player finely tuned.

That matrix of creation requires the full awareness and participation of human beings. Jesus was still human when he went up the mesa and stepped off into a vision of the Great Mystery behind all of creation. His presence represents our presence. As stewards of God, we are intimately involved in maintaining creation. Our task is not to be consumers of reality, but the protectors of Nature's balance. The second vision quest gives us our job description exactly as the Hopi envision it. We are the partners with all other living things to keep the beauty and purpose of life intact. It is a calling that requires commitment, even courage, especially in the face of adversity. But if we have faith, we will endure and do our job, no matter what.

In fulfilling our role in life we are part of an ancient covenant. The second vision quest is bookended by Moses and Elijah. Like the twin brothers of Hopi theology, Poganghoya and Palongawhoya, they embody the tradition that we uphold, a tradition of spiritual balance. As we preserve the health of the planet, we preserve the future. As we keep the air and water clean, the Earth unspoiled, the animals safe in their own homes, we make sure the cycles of life continue for all beings. We work in close relationship with the *katsinas*, the forces of life that surround us and on whom we must depend. Only by working with these embodiments of God's organic vision will we be able to do what we are called to do.

Life is inter-dependent. The sky depends on what happens with the sea. The sea with what happens on land. The smallest creatures can affect the largest. Our vision must be like the Hopi vision: a view of the natural world as it is transfigured into the image of the One who made it. As the second vision quest makes so clear, none of this can happen in a box. There is no one tradition or tribe that owns the Transfiguration. Not the Spanish friars. Not the Baptist schoolteachers. Not even the Hopi. The second vision of Jesus, as dazzling as it may be, ends in a fog of mystery, in the cloud of God's deepest thoughts: the place where our migration began and the destination to which it will return. Along that path of stewardship, we trust our ancestors. We work with the *katsinas*. We respect one another. And we never forget that we are always in the *kiva*. We are servants of the mystery, keepers of the hidden balance.

After his second vision quest, Jesus went back to healing people. He took his sacred power and put it to use, trying to keep things in balance. In the same way, after all of their struggles and sufferings, the Hopi carried on healing the world with their *kiva* ceremonies. They are still doing to this day what they believe they are called to do. They bear many scars. They have known many hardships. But the vision continues. The work of faith continues. It is not a Christian faith, although it tells us so much about what being a Christian means. Ironically, the most traditional Hopi demonstrate the most Christian values – not the distorted values of seventeenth century friars or nineteenth century missionaries, but the ancient values of the gospel, of the second vision quest of Jesus.

All things work together. Hopi tradition, as part of the Native Covenant, helps us to understand the meaning of Matthew's story. It allows us to see that story through the eyes of Hopi experience. It puts the Transfiguration into a different context, one that can renew our own commitment to get up and pay attention. Part of our work of maintaining balance is to make sure that what the Hopi people endured never happens again. The Hopi witness reveals the second vision quest as an affirmation for religious freedom, cultural integrity, and global identity. By defending their past, the Hopi show us our way to the future. For centuries they have had a rich and layered understanding of life. Now the rest of the world is starting to catch up. Hopi tradition is only now able to enlighten Christian scholarship. Perhaps in the years remaining in the Fourth World the Histatsinom will have much more to teach us.

Chapter 8

THE GARDEN

It is difficult for many Americans to realize that the United States Constitution was meaningless for much of the history between Native Americans and the Federal Government. As we have seen, a president of the United States could ignore the ruling of the Supreme Court when it came to the treatment of Native people; Native Americans were not granted American citizenship until 1924 when they were thought to be all but extinct; and it was not until 1978 that Native Americans were allowed to practice their religious beliefs, in spite of what the First Amendment to the Constitution had guaranteed to Americans for over two hundred years.

In 1978 Congress passed the American Indian Religious Freedom Act. It was a landmark piece of legislation for Native people because, for the first time in the four hundred year history between Europeans and Native Americans, the religious practices of Native nations were not banned. Native people were allowed to worship publicly. They could come out of the catacombs where they had been maintaining their religious beliefs in secret for fear of persecution.

The parallel to first-century Christians is hard to miss. Like Rome, the Federal Government had persecuted and suppressed Native religions in order to break the will of the Native American people to resist conquest. Native American prophets like Sitting Bull were imprisoned or executed. Religious dances like the Ghost Dance were prohibited under penalty of death. Traditional spiritual objects like the Hopi statues of the *katsinas* were systematically destroyed. Church operated boarding schools were established to remove Native children from their traditional religious culture and transform them into English speaking converts. In no other part of the world, except in

Hawaii where American churches were predominant, was there such a concerted, consistent, and conscious effort to eradicate an indigenous religious system. Not in India. Not in Africa. Not in any other area under colonial rule was there as intense a level of religious persecution as in the Americas.

The icon for this historic truth is Mount Rushmore. For generations before the coming of the colonizers, several Native nations (the Lakota, Cheyenne) held the Black Hills to be sacred. They went there for their vision quests. It was considered a "thin" place between this reality and the holy reality of God. The Black Hills were a natural cathedral for Native religion, a space not to be disrespected or violated, which explains why the Native nations who revered the Black Hills fought so hard to keep gold miners and gun slingers out of the area. Blasting into the rocks or setting up saloons on the Black Hills was like opening a strip club at the Vatican. Therefore, when the victorious Americans carved huge images of their leaders on the face of the hills, it was seen not only as a final insult but also proof that in the United States freedom of religion was not to be accorded to Native Americans.

Confronting this harsh reality of American history is not pleasant, but it is important because it is within the context of religious persecution that we discover the third vision quest of Jesus as the Native Messiah.

Among the ceremonies performed by the Native people who revered the Black Hills was one in particular that the American government forbade: the Sun Dance. Even today, after the American Indian Religious Freedom Act has lifted that ban, the Sun Dance remains a controversial subject. So deep is the memory of persecution that traditional Native Americans discourage any discussion about it. They ask non-Native people not to attend and they strictly prohibit any photographs or videos. On the other side of the controversy there are non-Native people who continue to find the Sun Dance barbaric, a kind of ritual of blood sacrifice. The Sun Dance, therefore, is an axis point for the historic relationship between the religious sensibilities of the American experience, both Native and non-Native alike.

Out of respect for my brothers and sisters who honor and perform the Sun Dance, I will be very circumspect in how I speak of it. I am not a Sun Dance person and I do not pretend to speak about it with any authority. However, I believe the theology of this sacred Dance, which is itself a vision quest, is crucial as it reveals the essence of the message and ministry of the Native Messiah, Jesus. Consequently, let me turn to a source we have used before, to Black Elk, and let his brief description of aspects of the Sun Dance that are public knowledge introduce us into a theological reflection. As a young man, just prior to the battle of the Little Big Horn, Black Elk observed preparations being made by his people for a Sun Dance and he offers us a clear picture of it in the context of a vision quest:

> *The next day the dancing began, and those who were going to take part were ready, for they had been fasting and purifying themselves in the sweat lodges, and praying. First, their bodies were painted by the holy men. Then each would lie down beneath the tree as though he were dead, and the holy men would cut a place in his back or chest, so that a strip of rawhide, fastened to the top of the tree, could be pushed through the flesh and tied. Then the men would get up and dance to the drum, leaning on the rawhide strip as long as he could stand the pain or until the flesh tore loose.*[1]

The tree Black Elk refers to is a small tree that was secured in the center of the dance ground circle, one that had been ceremonially chosen with great care and reverence. As in many other world religions, this symbol of the tree represented the axis mundi, the tree of life that is the link between earth and heaven. Of course, the aspect of the Sun Dance that caused Europeans such concern was not the tree, but the blood and pain endured by the dancers. This is the part of the dance that is at the heart of the controversy. What were these men who allowed themselves to be pierced and tied to a tree doing? What was their motivation and what was the meaning behind the dance?

The answer from the Native Covenant can be given in a single word: sacrifice. Men who participate in the Sun Dance do so because they have received a vision. They believe they have been given an opportunity to make a sacrifice of their own bodies, accepting the pain of piercing and torn flesh, in order to offer a blessing to their people. Their motivation is, therefore, a selfless act. They volunteer to dance out of an abiding love for their community. In the theology of the Sun Dance this noble gesture of love releases the power of healing into the whole nation. It allows the people to live and to prosper. It is an extreme form of the Good Medicine that sustains the traditional Native community.

The Europeans who banned the Sun Dance did not grasp the subtleties of this theology. They saw only the blood and the suffering of the dancers. They assumed it was a style of human sacrifice just short of ritual murder, but still a maiming of the body. Their anxious imaginations equated the Sun Dance with a ceremony of blood lust, something that would whip the hostiles into a frenzy, so they forbade it to be performed. From their viewpoint they had suppressed a primitive ritual designed to incite Native Americans to seek more blood. From the Native American viewpoint they had denied the whole nation the healing offered by a handful of faithful men who were responding to a call from God.

The suppression of the Sun Dance is important for us to consider because it so graphically illustrates the power of sacrifice in human society.[2] Sacrifice can be a fearful thing or a noble thing, depending on the spiritual vantage point of the culture observing it. Throughout human history, the single concept of sacrifice has had a profound impact on every religion and every people since our species first walked out of the savannahs of Africa. To do justice to the subject of sacrifice would take volumes. For the purposes of our study of the third vision quest of Jesus, I will only sketch the trajectory of this potent religious concept and let it bring us to a deeper appreciation of both the Native Covenant and the vision quest experience of the Native Messiah.

Beneath the plethora of anthropological and archeological examples of sacrifice in early human history going as far back as Paleolithic times there is a core concept that emerges: reciprocity. Whether the specific form of the act is animal sacrifice, the offering of grains, or a ritual performed on a sacred calendar, the principle behind all of these sacrificial acts is the same. At some point in the religious development of human consciousness was the recognition that our relationship to the divine, our connection along the axis mundi, was a reciprocal quid pro quo. Humanity developed the concept that if there were supernatural powers in control of the elements, they could be contacted, even influenced. The relationship was reciprocal. By our actions as human beings, we could effect change. In the moment of that revelation, human beings stopped being creatures who simply existed in a reactive state. We became conscious partners with the divine in altering reality. If we wanted rain, or a successful hunt, or good crops, or safe childbirth, there were things we could do to make that happen. We could pray. We could worship. We could sacrifice. These three primal spiritual concepts revolutionized our self-understanding. We were no longer passive recipients of whatever came along, but beings in a reciprocal relationship to the sacred. We had the ability to talk to the supernatural powers, we could show them we were aware of their power, and we could perform acts that effected their attitude toward us.

Religion, as a phenomenon of human culture, began with these three basic building blocks: prayer, worship, and sacrifice. Over time they have been used to create the most humble spiritual practices of hunter-gatherers or the most elaborate systems of postmodern societies. Like spiritual DNA, they exist as the foundational principles in shaping our religious practices. They are interrelated aspects of religion, often joined in practice or ritual, but each one is slightly different. Prayer is communication in a direct sense. Worship is experience in a broad sense. Sacrifice is offering in a specific sense.

Sacrifice is priming the pump of sacred reciprocity. It offers something in the hope of receiving something in return. It initiates contact.

By giving up what is possessed, sacrifice announces that the person or community is aware of its debt to the reciprocal relationship. It telegraphs our acknowledgment that we know that what we have is only by the gift of a higher power. Sacrifice also includes the message that we hope this reciprocal bond will continue, that we will continue to receive the blessings of the divine forces. Sacrifice, therefore, is a tithe. It is a ritualistic return of first fruits in order to secure a future with the same expectations.

Consider the layers of deeper meaning in this ancient idea. First, it implies that there is a consciousness at the other end of the transmission who can get the message and respond. Sacrifice presumes the existence of the divine in a conscious form. Secondly, it relies on a relationship of exchange. It is ritual barter. Third, it creates the phenomenon we call worship. It embodies the theological nature of the hierarchical relationship that brings human beings in humility to offer something to a Presence far beyond their control. Sacrifice is an admission that there is a higher will than the one exercised by the tribe of the human beings.

If we survey every religion in every culture in every time, we will find this same understanding at work. The idea of sacrifice is identical; only the form that it takes and the interpretation it receives varies. For some cultures, a very simple exchange was all that was required to make the holy relationship reciprocal: a coin tossed in a well or an offering of the first harvest. These small barters are still visible in our own Christian context in the Lenten season. Every Lent, Christians enter into a worshipful, reflective time. They seek to acknowledge the primacy of God in their lives. They give up eating chocolate. They pray more often. They curb their use of language. In essence, they sacrifice normal behaviors in order to keep the channel to God clear and conscious. Sacrifice is intentionality made manifest even in these small ways. It is a common part of our religious awareness.

Sacrifice, however, in the Christian context as well as that of other religions, has not always been as benign as giving up chocolate. The extremes to which people have gone (and continue to go) in the name of sacrifice is almost beyond cataloguing. We know the graphic examples of human sacrifice among the Aztec and the Celts; we know of royal burials in China and Egypt that included human sacrifice; we know of self-deprivations to an almost lethal level by Hindu mystics or Christian ascetics.

Even today we can observe the self-flagellation practiced by Iranian Muslims or the voluntary crucifixions of Filipino Christians. We still admire people like Julian of Norwich who walled herself up in a tiny room and Mahatma Gandhi who periodically almost starved himself to death. Viewed through both the historic and contemporary lenses of the extreme limits to which humans have taken the idea of sacrifice, the acts of the Sun Dance seem far less exaggerated than we might first have assumed. It is only one among a myriad number of ritual sacrifices that have been performed in human history and that continue to be performed to this day. What the men of Black Elk's time sought to accomplish was an ancient act of exchange with God. They believed, just as contemporary Sun Dancers still believe, that the sacrifice of their own bodies, of their own blood, will offer to God a small part of the life that God bestows on humanity. It is a return of life itself in humble acknowledgment of the power of the Creator. Ultimately, it is also a request, an appeal on behalf of humanity that God will continue to bless the people, and all creation, with a bounty of health and well-being.

The Sun Dance is the vision quest as sacrifice. It contains all of the classic elements of a vision quest. It demands a time of intentional and intense purification and preparation. It requires the presence of mentors and friends in a supporting role. It calls the person making the quest to a high and lonely place, in this case, to the very top of the tree of life where he can bring his lament on behalf of the people to God. What sets the Sun Dance apart from other forms of the vision quest is the element of sacrifice. It is not just a matter of forgoing food or water or sleep. It is an offering of the physical being of the person himself, a sacrifice of the substance of life to show respect to the source of life, God. Understood in this context, the Sun Dance is neither barbaric nor bizarre. It is an expression of an ancient tradition common to all human religions. It is a level of commitment to faith beyond that expected in some spiritual cultures, but not all. It is a form of worship that is a theological analogue to the Christian experience of sacrifice. It is an echo of the gospel story of the Native Messiah. It is an integral part of the third vision quest of Jesus.

Jesus was a Sun Dancer. In his third vision, he receives the call from God to make his sacrifice for the people. He is asked to voluntarily allow himself to be pierced for their sake. He knows that he will be taken to the tree and suspended there. There is no ambiguity about this vision. As the Native Messiah, he understands both the reasons and the consequences. From the perspective of the Native Covenant, the Sun Dance is the spiritual gateway to Christology. It explains the motivation of Jesus. It explains why God would extend this challenge to Jesus. It makes the third vision quest a pivotal time of decision for Jesus as he considers becoming a sacrifice: a giver of life, to the source of life, to make life continue.

Ironically, this crucial element of the Christian story is one of the reasons Christianity was banned by Rome. The persecution and martyrdom of Christians that drove them underground into the catacombs was justified because of stories like the death of Jesus on the cross.[3] These stories seemed barbaric and grotesque to educated pagans. The idea that a sacred person, much less God, would suffer in such a humiliating way was beyond the bounds of decency. It was primitive, almost as primitive in its blood lust as the other aspect of Christianity that the Romans abhorred: the ritual cannibalism of the Eucharist.

Like their American counterparts centuries later, the Romans felt justified in suppressing such a blood-splattered religion. Christians, of course, saw the Crucifixion and the Eucharist in a very different context, just as Native people saw the Sun Dance in a theological way. Both communities looked through the elements of sacrifice to a deeper meaning. When Native people first heard the account of the Crucifixion they were not appalled but affirmed. Here was the same act being performed by the Christian God that the United States had denied to them. Here was divine sanction for what their ancestors had taught them was a respectful way to make their lament to the Great Spirit in the Sun Dance. The only aspect of the story that seemed exaggerated to them was that Jesus had to die from his piercings. That seemed a sacrifice beyond what even the Sun Dancers expected.

Native American traditionalists are not alone in questioning the extent of the sacrifice required by God from Jesus. In contemporary Christian theology the doctrine of the atonement continues to be debated among scholars. The classic understanding is that Jesus died for our sins and became the sacrificial substitute for humanity. He took upon himself the wrongs of all human beings and allowed himself to be killed in their place. By so doing, Jesus made himself a sacrificial propitiation for our sins. His death offered us a chance to receive pardon. The reciprocal relationship with God was, therefore, reestablished. The sacrifice, even unto death, was necessary since the sins of humankind were so egregious to God.

This doctrine, which has been at the heart of Christian teaching for centuries, has been questioned by many Christian scholars. Once again, the notion of a blood sacrifice has come under scrutiny and many find the idea primitive or even shocking. Would God truly demand human sacrifice? Even though, in the case of the Christian understanding of the Incarnation, it is God in human form who is dying, many people still find the substitution theory unacceptable. They argue however we try to avoid the reality, Jesus, as a fully human person, suffered torment and death because God demanded it from him. What kind of loving God would do that?

It is not my purpose in this work to try to answer that question. As a Native American theologian, I only take note of the fact that the same issues that once justified the banning of the Sun Dance have reasserted themselves in Western theology. The Sun Dance is not a sacrifice to death, but its theology was unacceptable. The crucifixion of Jesus does represent a sacrifice to death, but its theology is perfectly acceptable. My goal in entering the theological dialogue is to return the Native Covenant to its rightful place in the realm of sacrificial theology through the Sun Dance. As a metaphor it offers us an opportunity to understand the nature of sacrifice from a vantage point other than that advanced by European tradition: from a perspective other than sin.

When read through the lenses of the Hebrew Covenant, the doctrine of the atonement makes sense as a rationale for the sacrifice of Jesus. Sin permeates the context of the Crucifixion. It begins, ironically enough, in another garden with the idea of an original sin by Adam and Eve. That garden story echoes throughout the rest of the Bible as God copes with human sin in a variety of ways, including a great number of bloody ways. Not only are whole cities and populations sacrificed because of sin, at one point the entire number of living creatures on the planet, save for one boatload of the faithful, are killed. The death of one person, even Jesus, seems completely rational given this enormous testimony to the depth and nature of sin in creation.

When read through the lenses of the Native Covenant, the idea of an atonement falters. Why? Because Native people believe they come from a different Garden. In their creation stories there is no original sin. Instead, First Man and First Woman usually appear as helpless creatures in need of support. They enter life in a state of "original lament." They are exactly what the vision quest theology embodies: pitiful beings crying out for a blessing. This appeal is heard and responded to in a variety of ways. The rest of the story, so to speak, is about how the many spirits and powers within creation come to the aid of human beings and help them cope.

From the perspective of Native tradition, the reciprocity of an atonement seems much less rational. A Native American Christology can easily embrace the notion of sacrifice by Jesus as a Sun Dancer; it can accept the suffering of Jesus as part of that experience because it understands the depth of the human lament, which is primal. It is more difficult, however, to comprehend why God would require an intentional sacrifice to the point of death. And yet, Jesus died. He sacrificed his life on the tree of life, giving away the most precious of all human possessions. Why did he do that? Why did that have to happen? Does the Native Covenant have any insights into this story of sacrifice by the Native Messiah? Yes, and the answers are in the garden.

In Matthew 26: 36–46, we read the story of the third vision quest of Jesus. Like all of the others, this one contains the traditional elements of a Native American vision quest. Jesus prepares himself (with a final farewell dinner with his friends). He goes to a high and lonely place, he has his friends with him for support, and he receives a vision. What is intriguing, however, is the location.

This is not a barren mountaintop. It is not a barren desert. The word garden from the Native American viewpoint is intriguing because Jesus chose to undertake this vision quest in a place lush with life. We do not need to imagine Gethsemane to be a manicured garden overflowing with flowers to get the point. Even if it was a place where olive trees grew in a small hilltop area, it was still garden-like in the presence (not the absence) of life. For a Native American Christian this symbolic location is crucial because our covenant is more focused on place than time. Location is everything. We are a people of sacred spaces.[4] Where things happened is far more critical to us than when they happened. The old stereotype of a vague reference to "many moons ago" is actually true for us when it comes to acknowledging our relative spiritual disinterest in chronology; but ask us where a sacred place is and we can tell you down to the exact location. Like, for example, the Black Hills.

The Native Messiah received his vision of death in the midst of life. The significance of this location is revealed when Jesus identifies his third vision quest as a "crying for a vision" beyond anything he has experienced before. "My soul is overwhelmed with sorrow to the point of death," he says.[5] From the Native viewpoint this tells us that the lament of the third vision quest is an ultimate expression of human need. As the Native Messiah, Jesus is asking God for a blessing of such proportions that it can fill every human desire. Just as in the Genesis accounts of First Man and First Woman, Jesus takes up the most ancient cry of the human species, the very primal reason for any sacrifice: an acknowledgment that humans are in need and that only God can meet that need.

The axis mundi for an appeal of this magnitude is not just a single tree of life, it is a whole forest of trees, a garden like the one human beings first stepped into at the dawn of our consciousness. Gethsemane is the vision quest when Jesus takes on his role as a Sun Dancer. He lifts the cry of humanity for a blessing that will fulfill the needs of the People, once and for all. The Garden vision quest, therefore, is cosmic in dimension. It is "to the point of death." No ordinary person could receive a vision to become a Sun Dancer to this level. The idea that one dance by one person could fulfill the deepest need of a crying humanity for all time is a sacrifice beyond precedent. It is traditional in its theology, but it is an extreme form of sacrifice not entertained by a human dancer. What makes the third vision quest of Jesus so extraordinary is that he understands his sacrifice to be in the context of messiahship. He is the Sun Dancer for all people, for all of creation, for all time. Through his Dance, all life will be blessed forever. His sacrifice will not be about a death for sin, but about a life for love.

From the Native American perspective, a crucial part of the meaning of the third vision quest is revealed in the strange interaction between Jesus and his friends. He has told them that he thinks this is the most important vision quest he will make. He has asked them personally to please stay with him in spirit because he is full of sorrow. He has asked them to be part of this quest with him. And what do they do? They fall asleep. As human beings, even though they are as close to Jesus as any friends can ever be, they cannot enter the vision. He is on his own. When Jesus receives his vision of the cup, when he begins to understand that his Sun Dance may cost him his life, he instinctively does what any Native person would do: he seeks to return to the community, to the people, to the tribe of the human beings. But the pathos of his third vision quest is the recognition that this is not going to be possible. If he truly wants to call down the ultimate blessing on all of life, then he is going to have to go to the tree alone.

Nothing could be more frightening for a Native person. The anguish of the Garden vision is not about death. It is about being alone. As the Native Messiah, what Jesus must struggle with is isolation. His friends are literally not there. They are asleep, gone during his most critical hour. They cannot do what he must do: make a sacrifice so profound that it will turn even the grave into a garden. Essentially, in Gethsemane during his third vision quest, Jesus understands that for him it has become a good day to die.

In traditional Native American culture, people did not fear death. In fact, they often prepared songs to sing while facing death, welcoming it as a part of life. A speech attributed to the Shawnee prophet, Tecumseh, may say it most clearly:

> So live your life that the fear of death can never enter your heart. Trouble no one about their religion; respect others in their view, and demand that they respect yours. Love your life, perfect your life, beautify all things in your life. Seek to make your life long and its purpose in the service of your people. Prepare a noble death song for the day when you go over the great divide . . . Show respect to all people and when it comes your time to die, be not like those whose hearts are filled with fear of death, so that when their time comes they weep and pray for a little more time to live their lives over again in a different way. Sing your death song and die like a hero going home.[6]

The Native Covenant taught people that this life was only part of the journey of reciprocity, that the garden continued on the other side not only for the tribe of the human beings but for all of creation. Consequently, more than once, Native people would startle Europeans with the calm dignity they exhibited as they faced death. In 1862 when the United States military carried out the largest mass execution in American history, hanging thirty-eight Dakota men at one time, these men went to their death singing. Why? Because they knew it was a good day to die.[7] They had watched their women and children starving to death; they had heard the lament of their people under American occupation when food supplies were withheld and hunting made impossible; they had stood up like warriors and fought back against overwhelming odds, against death itself, and, in their eyes, they had won. Even though they died, they had overcome death because they died so others might live.

The tradition of the "good day to die" is part of the Native Covenant. In Gethsemane, Jesus, like the Dakota warriors of 1862, realized it was his day to die so others might live. The vision of the cup was a singular vision. Only Jesus could drink from it because only Jesus, as the Native Messiah, could do what must be done to fulfill the original blessing of the Garden. For life to flourish, for justice to be possible, for healing to occur, for all of the things every human being who ever had lived or ever would live would ever need: Jesus would have to have the courage to step alone into the dance ground and raise his lament even "to the point of death."

The third vision quest, therefore, is not about a blood sacrifice to atone for sin. That interpretation of the vision can be argued from the Hebrew Covenant and Native American Christians are certainly free to embrace it if they choose to do so. However, from the view of the Native Covenant no such interpretation is required to understand the vision quest in the Garden. Jesus was not told by God that he must kill himself because human beings sinned through disobedience at some mythical point in the beginning of creation. From the Native experience of both God and life, that interpretation seems irrational, perhaps even barbaric. More logical from the Native Covenant view is the idea that humans began life in a Garden and to a Garden they seek to return. Our lament is not about sin, but about falling asleep. In our ignorance, pride, and rugged individualism we have made barren the Garden of God. This indictment is important to maintain in the Native Covenant because it illustrates a theology of sin from the Native American tradition. As we mentioned in chapter three, there is an understanding of reconciliation in Native tradition. People who wish to portray Native American traditional religion as being childlike in spiritual innocence and free of the heavy-handed Western preoccupation with sin have tried to mythologize the Native Covenant as having no concept of sin at all.

This is not true. Native spiritual tradition does understand the notion of sin. Native American people, like all human societies, have codes of conduct, ethics, morality, a sense of wrong-doing. There are rewards and punishments for good and bad behavior. There is no need to maintain an exaggerated gloss of Native civilization as being without a notion of sin. The issue is to place sin into proportion and into context. If we are talking about some original sin that marked all of humanity as fallen from grace once and for all, then no, Native American tradition did not accept that idea. But if we are saying that human beings are capable of disrespecting the Creator through their callous treatment of life in this dimension, then yes, the Native Covenant would certainly acknowledge that kind of sinful behavior.

Perhaps the best illustration of this kind of sin in the Native Covenant is the story of how the Sacred Pipe came to the people. The Pipe is one of the most universal sacramental objects in Native America. It is used in both private prayer and ceremonies. The Pipe is the axis mundi made accessible to all people. Even in its construction, it is symbolic of Native Covenant theology. The stem is made from wood, from the tree of life itself. It is also made from the Earth, the bowl represents creation. The Pipe is decorated in a way that symbolizes the presence of all animal life. The tobacco represents all plant life. When Native American people pray with the Pipe, they are engaging every aspect of creation to honor and communicate with God.

This extraordinarily powerful spiritual object was brought to human beings, as the Lakota story tells it, by a divine figure in female form, the White Buffalo Calf Woman. She appeared one day to two Native men carrying the Pipe as a gift. They were out on the open prairie when she approached them; one of the men saw her not as a divine epiphany, but as a woman alone who could be raped. This man was struck dead on the spot:

> *The traditional story is that, long ago, there was a time of famine. The chief of the Lakotas sent out two scouts to hunt for food. While the young men travelled they saw a figure in the distance and as they approached, they saw that it was a beautiful young woman in white buck skin. One of the men was filled with desire for the woman. He approached*

her, telling his companion he would attempt to embrace the
woman, and if he found her pleasing, he would claim her
as a wife. His companion warned him that she appeared to
be a sacred woman, and to do anything sacrilegious would
be folly. The man ignored the other's advice. The companion
watched as the other approached and embraced the woman,
during which time a white cloud enveloped the pair. After a
while, the cloud disappeared and only the mysterious woman
and a pile of bones remained.[8]

This story contains an unmistakable element of sin. It demon-
strates a notion of divine retribution. It is a cautionary tale that we
would be hard pressed to miss. Therefore, it is obvious that Native
American tradition recognized sin as a part of life. Like the Hebrew
Covenant, the Native Covenant maintains a strong sense of what is
right and wrong. Native tradition calls human beings to high standards of ethical behavior. However, unlike the Hebrew Covenant,
Native American theology does not record an origin story that could
be used to justify human sacrifice.

From the Native perspective, sin is not the rationale and substitution is not the method of the third vision quest of Jesus. The vision
he receives asks him to risk something even more fearful than death.
Called to the tree of life to make his Sun Dance, Jesus realizes that he
is being asked to end life so that life can continue. He is to draw all
of life within himself, but when he does, it means he will be standing
in a void. To accept the vision, therefore, Jesus has to be prepared
to recognize his good day to die. He has to be willing to go all
the way in making his gift of life that others might live in health
and harmony. He is not dying for their sins. He is dying for their
blessing. In the reciprocity of life, things die that things may live. In
this cosmic reciprocity of all life, the holy bargain is that God will die
so that all creation may live. In a startling humility, God made the
rules that govern life and death, now God will abide by those rules.
God will fulfill the contract by stepping into the life cycle for the love
of creation.

The pathos of the Garden vision quest is not that Jesus is going to his death. It is that Jesus is going into exile. Isolation is what Jesus faces as the Native Messiah, a fate far worse than death for any Native person. The fearful thought of permanent exile is the cup from which Jesus is asked to drink. As we will see in the next chapter, Jesus will become an exile to include every life in his dance. To reach beyond the margins of creation, however, means being cut off from creation. The courage of Jesus is not in facing death, but in facing what it means to be alone. To restore all of creation, Jesus must step outside of creation. What he is about to do, he must do alone. His friends will be asleep to him. God will be asleep to him. In the deepest level of the Native Covenant, in order for all things to be, Jesus must venture where no things can be. The balance he will affect is between being and nonbeing. As the Native Messiah, he must enter the void to reach the ground of being.

No average human, even one inspired by a Sun Dance vision, could hope to fulfill a challenge like the one Jesus encounters in the Garden. Quite literally, he is being asked to go where no person has gone before. The Native Messiah wakes his friends with the intention of being true to the vision he has received in the Garden. He is going to step off the edge of the world into oblivion. He is going to face the death not only of the body, but of the spirit. He is going to the great Alone. He will make his Sun Dance to maintain the balance of all life for all time. Jesus let's himself be taken to hang from the tree. He sacrifices not only his life, but his fear. The piercing and the blood loss will be very real. The pain and the anguish will be felt. For God, it will be a good day to die.

Chapter 9

THE CROSS

In March 1617 Rebecca Rolfe died suddenly in England at Gravesend on the Thames River. She was only twenty-two years old, but already she had made a name for herself that would continue through history. In her brief lifetime she is credited with having risked her own life to save a person about to be executed, having an unrequited love affair as poetic as that of Abelard and Heloise, preventing a war, and being presented to the King and Queen of England as an Imperial Princess. Among her descendants were two First Ladies, the wives of Woodrow Wilson and Ronald Reagan, as well as the noted astronomer, Percival Lowell. She was buried in St. George's Church in Kent, England. Although her exact burial spot at the parish has been lost, a statue commemorating her stands in the churchyard. It honors her not only by her Christian name of Rebecca Rolfe, but also by her maiden name, Pocahontas.[1]

Who does not know her story? In the United States, at least, not many. Of all the Native American women of our national history, her name stands out above the rest. Far above the rest. She is a legend. Even if people do not know her complete story, they have a name recognition trigger for who she is: the Indian princess who saved Captain John Smith from execution at the hands of her own father, the great chief Powhatan. Her heroic deed, motivated by her love for a man about to die, has been immortalized in histories that began to circulate as early as the seventeenth century, in books, poems, songs, and most recently in a Disney animation.

The only other Native American woman who comes close as a runner-up to her fame, a kind of historic Miss Congeniality, is Sacajawea, the young woman who helped Lewis and Clark find the

Pacific Ocean. These two women are virtually alone in the public mind when it comes to naming famous Native American women. Both are remembered for befriending white men. Both are honored for having supported the efforts of European colonization and expansion. Both are considered heroic. In the case of Pocahontas, and probably Sacajawea as the spouse of a French Catholic fur trapper, a part of the story also includes their conversion to Christianity. Pocahontas was certainly a Christian. In fact, a painting by John Gadsby Chapman entitled "The Baptism of Pocahontas" hangs in the Rotunda of the United States Capitol in Washington, D.C.[2] It is a study in the myth making that surrounds the historic figure of Pocahontas. Commissioned by the United States government in 1837, the painting shows her dressed in white, kneeling demurely before the baptismal font in the church at Jamestown, Virginia, the earliest permanent English colony in the Americas. She is surrounded by members of her own family, by white colonists, and with her future husband, John Rolfe, standing behind her. The Anglican priest, Alexander Whiteaker, is looking up to heaven with his hand raised in benediction. One of her Native relatives seems to be leaning forward while others seem to look away. What is so striking about this painting is not only its imagery of a docile Native being "saved," nor its location in the very center of white American power, but its timing. It was commissioned at the height of the removal of Native nations from the United States on the Trail of Tears. It was painted and hung while thousands of Native Americans were being marched either to their deaths or to exile.

It is only one of the vast number of images that have portrayed Pocahontas and Sacajawea in everything from paintings to postage stamps, but it is a unique piece of the legendary narrative of Pocahontas because it freeze frames on the religious subtext of her myth. Chapman's painting, done at a time when Native nations were being illegally forced out of the United States, celebrates a famous Native American, a woman, and does so at the moment of her conversion to Christianity. Is this pure coincidence? Why would a painting of a Native woman's baptism make its way into the halls of

Congress? Native American women were almost invisible to the white men who ordered them marched out of their homes into exile. Why would these same Congressmen want to see a daily image of one of them hanging in the halls of power?

Part of the answer can be given in a single word: squaw.[3] This word, taken from the Algonquin languages common to the northeastern part of North America, appears in English usage only four years after the death of Pocahontas, in 1622. Although its original meaning was the generic term for woman,[4] it entered the English language as a racist and misogynistic word that denigrated not only Native American women, but also Native culture as a whole. Squaw implied that women in Native culture were ignorant slaves to their men; in turn, it offered a backhanded slur against Native men as lazy and brutish males who mistreated their own wives.

I never offer refutation for racist epithets, whether they are applied to my community or to other communities of color, since to do so might inadvertently lend these slurs even the smallest amount of credibility, but I do think it is vital for us to understand why language like this evolved in European colonial culture. As Pocahontas was being laid to her rest in Gravesend, Europeans back in her homeland were starting to use the word squaw. They were beginning to demean her Native sisters with this innuendo. Given the personification and popularity of Pocahontas as an icon of Native women's nobility, courage, and Christian faith, how did attitudes shift so quickly? Like most origins for racism in human relations, the root causes are widespread and deeply entrenched. However, given the historic circumstances between the English settlers and their Native neighbors at this time, we can make some fairly clear connections.

Among one of the most common practices of a dominant culture that seeks to subvert and control a target culture is the process of labeling. Oppressive cultures name their prey. In order to alleviate their guilt for destroying the lives of other human beings, participants in acts of cultural cruelty intentionally dehumanize their victims. Racial slurs are part of this process. They are designed to define the identity of the oppressed. By making that identity as negative as possible, the slurs provide indirect justification for the oppression. For example, in terms of the African American experience, for Christian colonists to publicly admit that they were forcing kidnapped children onto slave ships is a moral oxymoron that would be difficult to maintain. In the Native American context, for Christian politicians to admit that they were forcing helpless children onto a death march would not make their national history seem quite so uplifting. Therefore, these children must be given a different identity, a new name, one that masks their humanity and makes the acts of brutality against them seem less appalling.

An interesting twist to this process of dehumanization is the projection that often occurs unconsciously on the part of the oppressors. A simple psychological formula explains this phenomenon: we often accuse others of the very behavior we fear and dislike most about ourselves. At the time that the word squaw was becoming popular among Europeans, Native American women enjoyed a level of freedom and respect in their societies that their European counterparts could not imagine. Colonial women were still considered the property of their husbands; they had no voice in government or civil affairs; they were not accorded equal education; they had no recourse legally in abusive relationships. In the Native American cultures that were rapidly disappearing under European conquest, women were in a far better situation. In Native nations, where the word squaw simply meant woman, women could own their own homes, participate in the governance of their nation, and divorce their husbands while retaining all of their possessions and means of income. Native women were, in these and many others ways, in a far stronger social position than European women. They had economic, religious, political, and sexual options that would not be accorded to white women in the United States for another three hundred years.

The term squaw, therefore, is not based in reality, but in the projection of a racist culture that seeks to scapegoat another people in order to justify their extermination. Twenty years after Pocahontas died, the European settlers in Connecticut declared total war on the Pequot. They surrounded one of the main Pequot villages, set fire to it, and then gunned down all of the men, women, and children who ran out of the flames. To morally justify this type of ethnic cleansing, these Christian settlers needed to erase the humanity of the women and the girls they killed. Thinking of them as being somehow less than human helped as they pulled the trigger.

Racism, ethnic slurs, misogyny: these are tools of control and domination. Idealization, trivialization, and cooption: these are masks that cover the face of abuse. Native women in American history have been largely ignored, cruelly treated, and deeply maligned. At the same time, they have been turned into the poster children for the national myth. The process of colonialism that was played out in the seventeenth century has continued into the twenty-first century. Native women are still suffering far beyond any of their counterparts in American society. They suffer higher rates of physical attacks and rape than women from other culture groups in our society. The majority of these attacks come from non-Native men who find the legal jurisdictions of Indian reservations convenient loopholes to slip through in hunting women to abuse. Native women have higher rates of incarceration, often related to domestic violence. They have higher rates of substance abuse and suicide, clear markers for a female population undergoing enormous stress. And yet, they are almost invisible to the larger society. They suffer in the hidden rooms of racism where they are still portrayed as squaws, people who do not quite measure up to being considered real people. In the meantime, Pocahontas appears as a cartoon to delight and distract, to reassure and redefine, to mask and mythologize.

When I walked out onto a rooftop years ago, I was trying to understand if it was possible to be both an authentic Native American and Christian at the same time. Given the truth of our history in this nation, it is not hard to understand why the answer to that question is not self-evident. The evidence of racism against my people is not just an historical artifact. Consider what Amnesty International had to say about the level of violence against Native women today:

Sexual violence against Indigenous women in the USA is
widespread. According to US government statistics, Native

American and Alaska Native women are more than 2.5
times more likely to be raped or sexually assaulted than other
women in the USA. Some Indigenous women interviewed
by Amnesty International said they didn't know anyone in
their community who had not experienced sexual violence.
Though rape is always an act of violence, there is evidence
that Indigenous women are more likely than other women
to suffer additional violence at the hands of their attackers.
According to the US Department of Justice, in at least 86
per cent of the reported cases of rape or sexual assault against
American Indian and Alaska Native women, survivors
report that the perpetrators are non-Native men.[5]

What happened to the Pequot continues to happen today because
the basic forces at work are the same. As uncomfortable as it is for
us to admit, we live in a society that still operates with a colonial
mentality. Racism is all around us. Misogyny appears in court cases
every day. Women are the canaries in the mine of our national secret.
The treatment of our women is a bell weather sign for how well
we are caring for other members of our community: children and
elders, people with physical or mental challenges, people with different sexual identities.

As a Native American I am aware of the statistics that the women
of my community face each day. They are not invisible to me.
Therefore, I am confronted with the moral dilemma of my faith. Is
this injustice aided and perpetuated by Christianity? Is the Christian
faith part of the problem or part of the solution? The painting in the
Capitol building frames the issue: is the acceptance of Christianity by
Native Americans only window dressing for white racism, or is it a
fulfillment of our own ancient covenant with God?

To be honest, the anger I carried as a descendant of the Trail of
Tears left me doubting that I could keep my Native identity and be a
Christian. Vine Deloria's book did not create my crisis of conscience,
it revealed it. Like most Native Americans, I was fully aware of our
past history. The hypocrisy of idealizing Pocahontas while murdering

her sisters was too obvious. I did not want to be painted into that picture. I had more than enough justification for blaming Christianity as the chaplaincy to colonialism. It was only because of my vision of the crow that I did not abandon the Christian tradition of my people. I believed in my vision quest. Therefore, I held my own heart and history in a state of spiritual tension.

Finally, in the revelation of the four vision quests of Jesus, I found a path to wholeness, a path that took me through a process of discovery in the Christian scriptures. It showed me how a Native American can embrace the New Covenant of the Native Messiah, not as a mask for European colonialism, but as an authentic expression of his or her own liberation. In a surprising way, Pocahontas has become a symbol of that liberation: she and all of her unknown and unnamed sisters are central to the final vision quest of Jesus. They are the center of the vision of the Cross.

The fourth and final vision quest of Jesus is the vision of women. In Matthew 27:32–55 we are told Jesus goes up for the last time to a high and lonely place: Golgotha, the Place of the Skull. He has prepared for this moment his whole life. He has accepted that this will be a good day to die. He is ready to fulfill his role as the Native Messiah. All that remains to complete this experience as a traditional Native American vision quest is the presence of his mentors or friends.

In Native American terms, it is critical that these supporters of his quest be present. A vision quest is never a solo flight into a personal audience with God; it is always tethered to the ground of community. But where are the friends of Jesus at this most crucial moment? They have run away. Men are conspicuous in their absence. The gospel story tells us that the men who were supporters of Jesus fled when the authorities came into the Garden to arrest him. They do not appear again until the postlude of the resurrection narratives, only after the women have come to bring them out of hiding.

To appreciate the spiritual situation being acted out between Gethsemane and Golgotha, it is important to place these events into the context of the Native Covenant. In Native American tradition all things must be kept in a sacred balance. Like yin and yang, the contrasting principles of life are of primary concern. Light and dark, hot and cold, high and low: reality is maintained in a tension between opposites. This duality is not static, but dynamic. The renewal of life depends on these polar energies continuing to bring the dichotomy of existence into equilibrium.

Therefore, one of the reasons Native American women could never be "squaws" is because if they were life would be grossly out of balance. As in all things, the relationship between human beings had to be kept in harmony as well. Men had certain roles to play in life, women had certain roles to fulfill, but the important thing was that however different they might be, they must be equal on the sacred scales of God. One could not outweigh another. One could not oppress the other. All relationships had to be equal. Both genders had a spiritual authority. Both were empowered by God to be part of the whole. In fact, the levels of equilibrium accorded to the sacred archetypes of male and female were so finely tuned that the point of definition between them could be permeable. Like Polynesian cultures, many Native American cultures understood that there were three genders: male, female, and two-spirit.

In contemporary American society the emergence of transgender people into the public consciousness seems like something new. In Native American culture, it is something quite old. The traditional Native Covenant embraced the full spectrum of humanity; no one was excluded from the human family. Young and old, male and female, gay and straight, one spirit and two-spirit: these were all part of the seamless sense of Native community. Consequently, part of the balance included human beings who were male or female in body but the opposite in spirit. They were called "two-spirit people" and honored because they embodied this sacred spiritual balance so clearly in their own lives.[6]

This sophisticated concept of the human family in the Native Covenant helps to explain theologically why the male friends of Jesus deserted him in the Garden. As Jesus himself understood from his vision in the Garden, he was going to have to make his final vision quest without them. His male friends could not help him. They could not come with him. They were "asleep" to him. In other words, the power of the male spirit could not complete the circle. Another power, another balance, was needed.

Matthew 27:55–56 says, "Many women were there, watching from a distance. They had followed Jesus from Galilee to care for his needs. Among them were Mary Magdalene, Mary, the mother of James and Joses, and the mother of Zebedee's sons."

One of the most striking things about the story of the crucifixion of Jesus is the absence of men and the presence of women. However the story varies among the gospel writers, this single motif is repeated: the men ran away, the women stayed. There were, according to Catholic tradition, women like Veronica along the path to Golgotha. There were women on the hill where he was crucified. There were women at his tomb when he was resurrected. In the Synoptic gospels the women are portrayed as watching nearby; in John's story Jesus actually speaks to his mother who is standing below him. Women predominate the story of the fourth vision quest. They are everywhere.

From the perspective of the Native Covenant, there are reasons for this shift in the sacred balance of the story. In the earlier vision quests, angels and men had taken a part in the experience. There were *katsinas* at the first vision quest, and there were men at both the second and third quest. At this final and most crucial quest, however, it was time for women to be primary. What is crucial to comprehend theologically is that this was not because everyone deserved a turn; the principle of spiritual balance in the Native Covenant is far more subtle. The physical presence of women as participants with Jesus in this most profound vision quest is a signal that their spiritual authority is absolutely necessary. The sacred power of women is entering into the story, into the vision, just as male figures like Moses and Elijah could be seen in an earlier quest.

Women are not just accidental bit players in a male story. They are spiritually present because they have a weight of authority men do not have; without them, things would be out of balance. Women complete the circle of sacred vision. They infuse the vision with the

holiness of their being, with the archetype of the female that is essential to the order and harmony of all creation. These women are there
for a reason. Their "caring for the needs of Jesus" is more than just
doing the cooking and washing up. They are not there as "squaws";
they are there because they are part of a moment no male could fulfill. The women are in this quest because the vision Jesus receives on
the cross is of cosmic significance. Just as he had understood in the
Garden, it is a vision that is beyond what any other male dancer can
achieve. It calls down a blessing so overwhelming that it not only
changes his name: it changes his being.

On the cross Jesus becomes a Two-Spirit Messiah.

Many years after this vision quest, after the crucifixion, when
the apostle Paul wrote his letters to the new Christian communities
springing up all around the Mediterranean, he told them "in Christ
there is no male or female."[7] As an intuitive interpreter of the Jesus
story from the viewpoint of the Native Covenant, he got it exactly
right.

The man, Jesus, had made the commitment to make this final
quest, knowing it would be his good day to die, because he was
willing to take on the role God had shown him in his Garden vision:
he was to become something no one else could become, a universal
Sun Dancer who would be taking into himself the spirit of every
person who ever lived, dying that they might live, sacrificing for
their well-being. This vision quest would establish balance for all of
humanity, but for that to happen the "I" had to become the "we";
Jesus had to literally embody the spirit of the whole tribe of the
human beings. The "he" had to also be the "she." The finely tuned
lines of demarcation between us as the children of God had to be so
perfectly calibrated that both spirits are present at once. Perfect harmony is achieved.

In the person of Jesus, all of humanity is drawn together. The
sacred balance is perfected. What has been out of balance in our
relationships in the past now has a chance of returning to a holy
equilibrium. Racism, misogyny, classism, homophobia, exploitation,
and injustice of any kind now can be reconciled through the Native

Messiah. His healing vision, his Good Medicine, can reach the whole human family, but only if it is no longer "his," but "ours."

In the Native Covenant, the fundamental priority for maintaining balance in all relationships creates a vision of community where the "we" is always more important than the "I." By becoming a Two-Spirit Messiah on the cross, Jesus physically embodies that principle. He is male; he is female; he is both spirits combined. The transition he makes is one that no other single male or female could make. He enters a vision so powerful that through it he becomes what the Greeks called the Christ. In Native American theology, that sense of Christology, of universal inclusiveness, is what we mean by the Two-Spirit Messiah. It is a crucial transition because it explains both the nature and the purpose of this final vision quest.

In order to be the universal Christ, Jesus must take into himself the fullness of humanity on the cross. He must become humanity. On the cross, he is male and female; he is Two Spirit. In this way, he takes into himself the nature and experience of every person, including our experience of deep pain. As a Two Spirit Messiah, Jesus experiences the exploitation and abuse suffered by human beings who are targeted by the societies in which they live. During his crucifixion he is, for example, a Native woman; he feels what it means to be called a squaw.

The fact that Jesus becomes the marginalized person, the targeted person, explains why Matthew's story contains so many instances of Jesus being mocked on his way to the cross. During his interrogation and torture he is mocked by the soldiers when they put a robe and crown of thorns on him. They spit on him. He is mocked with the sign "this is the king of the Jews" placed over his head on the cross. Matthew is careful to record each and every instance of this humilia-tion. He tells us "those who passed by hurled insults at him," telling him to "come down from the cross, if you are the Son of God."[8] Matthew goes on to tell us "in the same way the chief priests, the teachers of the law and the elders mocked him," saying, "He trusts in God. Let God rescue him now if he wants him." To complete the abuse poured on Jesus, Matthew includes the thieves in his story telling us "in the same way the robbers who were crucified with him also heaped insults on him."[9]

It may be that this series of public humiliations adds to the pathos of the crucifixion story from the vantage point of European styles of theology. If the purpose of the crucifixion is understood as Jesus dying for our sins, then these incidents underscore the sinful nature of humanity in being cruel to Jesus and rejecting him. From the perspective of Native American theology, however, the insults take on a more central and nuanced place in the fourth vision quest narrative. First, they indicate that as the Native Messiah, Jesus is suffering a fate worse than death. Dying is not the pivotal point for the Native Covenant. Exile is the issue. When Matthew tells us that the "chief priests, the teachers of the law and the elders mocked him," he is telling us in Native terms that the whole community has turned against Jesus. In Native American community, if the elders reject you, then you are truly banished from the tribe of the human beings.

The great suffering Jesus endures is this sense of exile, one that he feels so deeply in the lament of his last vision quest that he even cries out to God, "Why have you forsaken me?"[10] This cry of the Native Messiah is the most chilling moment of the crucifixion. In the heart of his vision, Jesus faces the ultimate exile. He must go to the very limits of endurance that any human being can suffer. In order to fulfill this quest, in order to transcend individuality to embody Native community, in order to literally "become" all members of the tribe of the human beings, Jesus must experience the depth of the lament of any person who has ever felt rejected by their community.

Unlike the interpretation of the crucifixion in Christian theologies that believe Jesus had to die as a blood sacrifice of atonement, the Native American Christian view is that he had to live in a new way in order to heal the whole circle of humanity. He had to become the "we" to the farthest limit of that definition. In order to call back every person from exile, he had to go where they are, on the very margins of society, cut off and alone, rejected and abused. He had to feel what homosexual people feel when they are rejected; what people of color feel when they are demeaned; what people with physical challenges feel when they are ignored; what any human being who has ever been abused feels like to the core of their being.

The death of Jesus, therefore, was not required by God to stave off divine retribution against a fatally flawed humanity that deserves eternal punishment, but an act of self-sacrifice and love so profound that it brought enough Good Medicine in the world to heal the broken hoop of the nation for every person on earth.[11] The fourth vision quest restored the most essential aspect of creation: kinship.

Racism destroys kinship. Sexism destroys kinship. Classism destroys kinship. Homophobia destroys kinship. When human beings exile other human beings from the circle of life, they are breaking the hoop of the human nation, tearing apart what God has created. The sin of humanity is not a lifetime stain inherited from mythic ancestors who disobeyed a rule, but a daily choice made by all of us in the here and now, in living relationships that embody our kinship.

In the beginning of the seventeenth century, European Christians had a choice. They could have acknowledged kinship. They could have resisted the temptation of racism that pretended that one kind of human being is better than another. They could have worked with Native nations to establish a new community, one that would have shared resources and helped each to grow. Perhaps part of this exchange could have offered European women a more respected place in their own society. The liberation of the human spirit among American women could have occurred centuries ago. The fact that these choices were not made illustrates why the sacrifice of the Native Messiah is so profound. The message of his vision quest, the reason he chose his good day to die, and the point of his becoming a Two-Spirit embodiment of all people is so we might see more clearly the choice before us. He came and died not for our sins, but for our sight. He came that we might have his vision.

Native American women are still standing beside the cross of history. They are still bravely facing the suffering of humanity. They are living witnesses to the death caused by exile, rejection and abuse. By their presence they are calling racism, sexism, classism, colonialism, and homophobia into account. They are insisting that no one can be left out of the family of human beings. Their spirit is the spirit of life. They are the life bearers of the People. Jesus, as the Native Messiah, the Christ, is their sacred sister. Christ is who they are. Christ, the Two-Spirit Messiah, who is neither male nor female but both in one person, is the living vision of equality before God that is the birthright of every human being. The place of women at the cross, therefore, is the antithesis to the image of Pocahontas at the font. They are not there as handmaidens to the Lord; they are not there to be redeemed from the sinfulness of their being; they are not the symbols of a mythic fall from grace that has cursed humanity. In Native American theology, they are there to birth the spiritual transition of a human being from this reality into the reality of God. They are the midwives of the Christ.

Pocahontas is a visual aide for the fourth vision quest of Jesus because she symbolizes why he went to the cross to make his final lament. Millions of Native American women have lived and died in obscurity. Their stories are untold and unrecognized, but we know from history the truth of what they endured. They were targeted by white men for extermination. They were abused and exploited. They went into exile and suffered. They are still referred to by a slur that demeans their dignity and denies their reality. The poster child for their experience is a cartoon character, a subservient female receiving her redemption from white men.

In this context, Pocahontas and Sacajawea stand for every person who has ever been exploited and marginalized by a dominant society. What happened to Native women happened to other women of color. It happened to men of color. It continues to happen to a great many people of all ethnic and religious backgrounds. It happens to people of all ages and both genders. It happens to people who are gay or lesbian. It happens to transgender human beings. It happens across lines of economic class and social privilege. The list is long, but the story is very much the same.

From the Native American viewpoint, Jesus did not have to come to die for the actions of First Man and First Woman. Jesus had to become the Native Messiah to show us, once and for all, that we are all the same. We are the tribe of the human beings. We are family. We are related. As self-evident as that may seem to some of us, it is an historic recognition that has yet to be achieved. The statistical truth of the experience of Native women is symbolic of the racism and exploitation that continue on a daily basis around us. Humanity still suffers daily and deeply from religious intolerance, racial violence, and endemic warfare.

The most fundamental lessons of kinship seem to elude us. Therefore, the Native Covenant and the Christian theology it supports becomes critical. It becomes life-giving. It becomes liberating. Native American Christian theology shifts the focus of the fourth vision quest from individual salvation to communal redemption. It moves our attention away from the mantra that Jesus came to die so "I" might be forgiven and inherit eternal life. It opens up the vision that Jesus came to live as we live, all of "us," even the most marginalized, so that we might finally learn to love one another and live in harmony with creation as the tribe of the human beings. The fourth vision quest is not about something Jesus did for "me"; it is about who he became for "us."

The fourth vision quest of Jesus ends with his death. He releases his spirit back to God. Matthew, like a good Native American theologian, tells us that "the earth shook and the rocks split," a sign of the Emergence of life from the womb of the Earth. Like a Choctaw elder he tells us that "the tombs broke open and the bodies of many holy people who had died were raised to life . . . they went into the city and appeared to many people,"[12] which from the Choctaw tradition would symbolize that those isolated in individual burials, exiled from the family of the People, were restored to the communal life, both now and in the life to come. Even the centurion, the white colonist with the gun, recognizes the power of the vision and proclaims "surely he was the Son of God."[13]

At this point, the vision quest cycle is complete. As a human being, Jesus has undertaken the quest four sacred times. He has made a circle, acknowledging each of the four cardinal points of the divine compass. He has walked with the spirits, with men, with women, and

now he walks with God. The resurrection, therefore, is not an epi-
logue to the crucifixion as a miraculous event, a kind of proof that
Jesus is God. From the Native American theological viewpoint it is
a symbolic return from exile. The Two-Spirit Messiah comes out of
the single grave to rejoin the tribe of the human beings. The isolation imposed not by death, but by human behavior, is rolled back.
The vision of the Christ is released into the world. Because Jesus can
live in a two-spirit way, embodying all people in one reality, so can
we. We can turn back from the exile of ego to be part of the family,
to live in kinship and love. The resurrection points us in that direction. It means that the vision quest continues, for each one of us, as
we seek to follow the Native Messiah in our daily lives. The reason
these stories show Jesus in a human form, breaking bread with other
people and talking with them, is to ground the vision into the communal life of the people.

Easter is not about eternal life for the few who have a personal
relationship to Christ. That attitude would so narrow the vision
quests of Jesus as to put them in a box of human ego. Easter is
about daily life for the many who need to have a personal relationship with one another because until we do see one another as related
we will go on perpetuating the suffering of our human family. Easter
is not about a few of us getting to escape this sorrowful situation
because we grabbed the coattails of Christianity and made it out
before the big collapse. Again, the ego such a notion would imply
and the lack of acceptance of responsibility for human reality is unacceptable from the Native American perspective. What Easter offers us
is a way to live into our accountability for one another in the here
and now. What happens in the afterlife is completely the gift of God.
We have no control over it and no need to worry about it. Our task
is to maintain the balance of life in this dimension. Our corporate
responsibility is to be aware that as it "happens to the least of these,
it happens to me."[14] In Native Christian theology the Resurrection
opens the door to our tomb, not by promising us eternal life for
ourselves, but by taking us out into the light to see one another
more clearly.

In the four vision quests of Jesus we clearly see the Good Medicine that can heal our world. If we honor the one God of all of our covenants, if we have no exiles from the tribe of the human beings, if we live in harmony with all of our relatives throughout creation, and if we sacrifice for the sake of justice, then we will live. We will walk in the blessing way, surrounded by our ancestors, journeying with the spirits from all four sacred directions, toward a tradition that will become our future. The Native Messiah shows us the way. The Two-Spirit God calls us with a voice that speaks every language. We need to be awake now. We need to be preparing ourselves. We need to gather our friends and our teachers. It is time to go to a high place, to a sacred place, where we can see more clearly. Something holy is about to happen. Something that will change our name.

Notes

INTRODUCTION   The Circle

1. The debate over when and how the Western Hemisphere was first discovered,
explored, and settled is an ongoing academic controversy. I have chosen to press the
point from a Native American viewpoint by claiming an ancestry in North America
of 30,000 years. Is this possible?

> In 2014, the Indian Country Today Media Network, one of the major
> online sources for contemporary Native American issues, ran a five
> part series on the Bering Strait theory, the popular notion that ancient
> peoples walked across a land bridge from Asia into the Americas
> during the last Ice Age, somewhere between 10,000 and 15,000
> years ago. These articles are archived at Indian Country Today:
> http://indiancountrytodaymedianetwork.com/2014/07/04/
> bering-strait-theory-pt-4-indisputable-facts-artifacts-155659
>   Written by Alex Ewen, this study questioned many of the classic
> assumptions about when and how Native people first came to the
> Americas. In Part Four of his series, for example, published online
> on 7/4/2014, Ewen highlighted this kind of evidence in his article
> "The Indisputable Facts of the Artifacts":
>   During the construction of a dam in Lewisville, Texas the remains
> of a bison were uncovered in 1949, leading to a series of excavations
> that continued until the dam was finished and the site inundated
> in 1957. The excavations, as archaeologists Wilson W. Crook, Jr.,
> and R.K. Harris wrote in the journal *American Antiquity*, "yielded
> remains of more than 21 hearths of an ancient campsite of early man.
> An extensive Upper Pleistocene fauna has been recovered, much of
> it actually burned within the hearths themselves, and the remainder
> closely associated with camp refuse, along with certain distinctive arti-
> facts." What created a stir was that two of the hearths were radio-
> carbon dated at more than 37,000 years old.

My point in saying that my ancestors have been here for thirty thousand years is
not to claim any scientific position as being "indisputable," but to encourage us to
focus on the dispute itself. There is as much politics as science in the debate. Ewen,
along with many other Native writers, has argued that the ten thousand to fifteen
thousand year timelines usually associated with Native settlement (especially through

supposed passageways across the North American ice cap of those times) are often accepted because they support a Euro-centric attitude that still seeks to diminish the Native "claim" to the Americas. Concerns about racism have been very much a part of this debate.

My thirty-thousand year old pedigree is an intentional invitation to anyone who reads my book to study this ongoing debate both critically and carefully.

To engage the land bridge evidence, I would recommend Dan O'Neill, *The Last Giant of Beringia: The Mystery of the Bering Land Bridge* (New York: Basic Books, 2005). To become familiar with some of the challenges made to the Bering Strait concept: Barry Fell, *America B.C.* (New York: Times Books, 1976). To consider more contemporary theories that have engaged debate: Gavin Menzies, *Who Discovered America? The Untold History of the Peopling of the Americas* (New York: William Morrow, 2013). But most of all, continue seeking out the rational threads between all of these arguments that lead you to an awareness that Native people have an ancient presence in this part of the world that truly needs no validation to give them the right to speak with spiritual authority about their own homeland.

1   The Quest

1. Vine Deloria, Jr., *God Is Red* (Golden: Fulcrum Publishing 2003).
2. To learn more about the history of the Choctaw Nation, see: Angie Debo, *The Rise and Fall of the Choctaw Republic* (Norman: University of Oklahoma Press, 1975).
3. The "Trail of Tears" is the term used to describe the forced removal of many Native American nations from the eastern United States. See: Grant Forman, *Indian Removal: The Emigration of the Five Civilized Tribes of Indians* (Norman: University of Oklahoma Press, 1974) and Anthony F.C. Wallace, *The Long, Bitter Trail: Andrew Jackson and the Indians* (New York: Hill and Wang, 1993).
4. To understand AIM in its original context, you can begin with: Dennis Banks and Richard Erodes, *Ojibway Warrior: Dennis Banks and the Rise of the American Indian Movement* (Norman: University of Oklahoma Press, 2005). The co-founder of AIM was: Russell Means, *Where White Men Fear to Tread: The Autobiography of Russell Means* (New York: St. Martin's Griffin, 1995). For an overview of the whole time period try: Paul Chaat Smith and Robert Allen Warrior, *Like A Hurricane: The Indian Movement from Alcatraz to Wounded Knee* (New York: The New Press, 1997).
5. The mid-1960s to mid-1970s was an era of "taking sides." For example, I was active in the Native American right's movement, which labeled me as a "radical"; however, in my seminary, I was called "conservative" because in a classroom discussion I began a sentence by describing the Western cultural attitude toward women as male dominant; I got cut off before I could finish that sentence and given the label as a conservative who opposed women's ordination. Ironically, the last part of what I never got to say was that my own Choctaw culture is matrilineal and that my people had been ordaining women as spiritual leaders for centuries. This context of "taking sides" is important because within the Native American community there is still a strong sense of division between being a Christian or a Traditionalist. Unlike my seminary experience, we need to listen carefully to one another as this dialogue continues.

6. James George Frazer, *The Golden Bough: A Study in Magic and Religion* (New York: Oxford University Press, 2009).

7. See: Claude Levi-Strauss, *Myth and Meaning: Cracking the Code of Culture* (New York: Schocken, 1995); Mircea Eliade, *Shamanism: Archaic Techniques of Ecstasy* (Princeton: Princeton University Press, 2004); Carl Gustav Jung, *Man and His Symbols* (New York: Dell, 1968); and Joseph Campbell, *The Hero with a Thousand Faces* (Princeton: Princeton University Press, 1973). There are many different editions of Campbell's work, but this is the one I first read in 1973 when I began my vision quest.

2 The Vision

1. John G. Neihardt, *Black Elk Speaks* (Lincoln: The University of Nebraska Press, 1979), xiii.
2. *Ibid.*, xvi.
3. *Ibid.*, 17.
4. *Ibid.*, 18.
5. *Ibid.*
6. *Ibid.*, 19.
7. *Ibid.*, 20.
8. *Ibid.*
9. *Ibid.*
10. *Ibid.*, 24.
11. *Ibid.*
12. *Ibid.*, 27.
13. *Ibid.*, 21.
14. *Ibid.*, 22.
15. *Ibid.*, 23.
16. *Ibid.*
17. *Ibid.*, 36.
18. There is not an abundance of materials on the many prophets of the Native tradition. One direct source is: Arthur Caswell Parker, *The Code of Handsome Lake, the Seneca Prophet* (London: Forgotten Books, 2008). David Edmunds takes a biographical approach: David Edmunds, *Tecumseh and the Quest for Indian Leadership* (White Plains: Pearson, 2006). For an overview see: Alfred Cave, *Prophets of the Great Spirit: Native American Revitalization Movements in Eastern North America* (Lincoln: University of Nebraska Press, 2006).
19. The Great Law of Peace is among one of the best known examples of how Native visionary tradition translated into the pragmatic experience of community-building among Native nations and how the vision of Native people helped to shape the United States Constitution. See: Gregory Schaaf, *The. U.S. Constitution and the Great Law of Peace: A Comparison of Two Founding Documents* (Santa Fe: Center for Indigenous Arts and Cultures, 2004) and William N. Fenton, *The Great Law and The Longhouse* (Norman: University of Oklahoma Press, 2010).
20. Neihardt, *Black Elk Speaks*, 138.
21. *Ibid.*, 140.
22. *Ibid.*, 140.

23. *Ibid.*, xiii.
24. *Ibid.*, 1.

3 The Voice

1. John 11:40 (All of the biblical citations in this book come from The New International Version published by Zondervan in 1986).
2. John 20:29.
3. Red Jacket's speech to the missionary is almost apocryphal in American history, but the character of Red Jacket was very real. He embodied the reasoned resistance of traditional Native people to the pressure of religious colonization. You can find out more in: Arthur C. Parker, *Red Jacket: Seneca Chief* (Lincoln: Bison Books, 1998).
4. Matthew 11:4–6.
5. Soren Kierkegaard, *Fear and Trembling* (Seattle: CreateSpace Independent Publishing Platform, 2011).

4 The Messiah

1. The primary source I used for the story of Wovoka in this chapter was: Michael Hittman, *Wovoka and the Ghost Dance* (Lincoln: University of Nebraska Press, 1997). Out of print but still available is also: Paul Dayton Bailey, *Wovoka, The Indian Messiah* (Tucson: Westernlore Press, 1957).
2. My primary source for the 1890 massacre at Wounded Knee is: James Mooney, *The Ghost Dance Religion and Wounded Knee* (Mineola: Dover, 1973).
3. One of the most succinct descriptions of the United States military strategy against the Plains nations, and the role General William Tecumseh Sherman played in it with his scorched earth policy of killing the buffalo, can be found from the Smithsonian. In an article published online at Smithsonian.com on July 17, 2012, Gilbert King details how this planned extermination was formulated and carried out: http://www.smith sonianmag.com/history/where-the-buffalo-no-longer-roamed-3067904/?no-ist
4. Mooney, *The Ghost Dance Religion and Wounded Knee*, 869.
5. The Medals of Honor was awarded to twenty of the soldiers who participated in the Wounded Knee massacre. See Dana Lone Hill's article in the American edition of *The Guardian*, posted in their American edition on February 18, 2013. In the article, entitled "The Wounded Knee Medals of Honor Should Be Rescinded," Dana Lone Hill explains how the American Congress has acknowledged the event as a massacre, but has not been willing to withdraw the medals it awarded to the perpetrators. See: http://www.theguardian.com/commentisfree/2013/feb/18/massacre-wounded-knee-medals-honor-rescinded.
   An even more thorough description of this history can be found at the Nebraska State Historical Society archives: http://nebraskahistory.org/publish/publicat/his-tory/full-text/NH1994MedalsWKnee.pdf
6. "In 1924 historian-actor Tim McCoy delivered Wovoka by limousine to the set of a movie he was making in northern California. There he was treated with absolute reverence by Arapahos who had been hired for the film." This is how the online

Encyclopedia of World Biography briefly describes the encounter between silent film star Tim McCoy and Wovoka. There is an historic photo of the two of them in several other sources. See: http://www.ghostdance.com/history/history-wovokaewb. html,

7. Matthew 26:26.
8. Matthew 26:27.

5   The Clown

1. Matthew 3:5.
2. Matthew 3:10.
3. Matthew 11:2.
4. Footnoting the terms *koshare* and *heyoka* offers me the opportunity to make a critical point about the Native American attitude toward the definitions imposed on our traditions by Western anthropologists and authors. We feel that a great deal of what has been written about our culture is bogus. In this book, I try to strike a balance between providing sources for my work and showing deep respect for the sanctity of Native religious life. In this case, I choose not to footnote these two terms because, as a Native person, I believe much of the written documentation is suspect.
5. Matthew 3:12.
6. "Although the extended family is typical of American Indians, its core is quite different from that of the dominant culture. Family therapist Terry Tafoya (1989) explains: 'In many Native American languages, cousins are referred to as brothers and sisters.'" This succinct explanation of the Native American tradition that would allow us to describe John and Jesus as "brothers" can be found in: Monica McGoldrick, Joe Giordano, and Nydia Garcia Preto, eds., *Ethnicity and Family Therapy* (New York The Guilford Press, 2005).
7. The "trickster" figure is universal. Here are two sources for the Native American variation: Franchot Ballinger, *Living Sideways: Tricksters in American Indian Oral Traditions* (Norman: University of Oklahoma Press, 2006) and Richard Erdoes, *American Indian Trickster Tales: Myths and Legends* (New York: Penguin Books, 1999).
8. The "give-away" is a custom widely recognized in Native American traditional culture, but one very simple and clear explanation was offered by the Native American artist, Cheryl Davis, at her online site: https://bymyart.wordpress. com/2007/12/27/native-american-give-away-tradition/

6   The Wilderness

1. John R. Swanton, *Source Material for the Social and Ceremonial Life of the Choctaw Indians* (The University of Alabama Press, 2001): 180.
2. *Ibid.,* 181.
3. Patricia Galloway, *Choctaw Genesis 1500–1700* (Lincoln: The University of Nebraska Press, 1995): 334.
4. *Ibid.,* 85.

5. Two recent books help to underscore the depth of this paradigm shift between cultures: Jace Weaver, *The Red Atlantic: American Indigenes and the Making of the Modern World, 1000–1927* (Chapel Hill: University of North Carolina Press, 2014) and Charles C. Mann, *1491: New Revelations of the Americas Before Columbus* (New York: Vintage, 2006).
6. David Edmunds, *Tecumseh and the Quest for Indian Leadership* (London: Pearson, 2006).
7. The Choctaw Nation of Oklahoma maintains an online history, including information about the early missionary movement. This comment about the schools comes from that archive: http://www.choctawnation.com/history/post-removal-government-treaties/cyrus-byington/
8. A description of this period in Choctaw history can be found in: Angie Debo, *The Rise and Fall of the Choctaw Republic* (Norman: The University of Oklahoma Press, 1975).
9. Anthony F.C. Wallace, *The Long, Bitter Trail: Andrew Jackson and the Indians* (New York: Hill and Wang, 1993).
10. Andrew Jackson's exact words are a subject of debate, but the *New Georgia Encyclopedia* captures the essence of it in an online archived article by Tim Alan Garrison of Portland State University, 10/1/2014: http://www.georgiaencyclopedia.org/articles/government-politics/worcester-v-georgia-1832
11. There are many good studies of the Trail of Tears, but here is a classic: Grant Forman, *The Emigration of the Five Civilized Tribes of Indians* (Norman: University of Oklahoma Press, 1974).
12. Timothy R. Pauketat, *Cahokia: Ancient America's Great City on the Mississippi* (New York: Penguin Books, 2010).
13. A more thorough description of Native American family systems can be found in: Monica McGoldrick, Joe Giordano, and Nydia Garcia Preto, eds., *Ethnicity and Family Therapy* (New York: The Guilford Press, 2005).
14. For a more in-depth look at traditional Choctaw clan systems, see: H. B. Cushman, *History of the Choctaw, Chickasaw, and Natchez Indians* (Norman: University of Oklahoma Press, 1999).
15. Matthew 4:4.
16. Matthew 4:7.
17. N. Scott Momaday, *The Way To Rainy Mountain* (Albuquerque: University of New Mexico Press, 1976).
18. Matthew 20:26.
19. Matthew 4:10.

7   The Mountain

1. I am extremely cautious in offering citations for this chapter because it deals with a Native American community that has been much abused and is understandably protective of their traditions, the Hopi. The background book that I share here is not without its critics, but it remains as a general reference in common use, so read it accordingly: Frank Waters, *The Book of the Hopi* (New York: Penguin Books, 1977).
2. Ditto the cautions mentioned above, but these works speak to the depth of the Hopi experience: Edmund R. Nequatewa, *Truth of a Hopi: Stories Relating to the*

Origin, Myths and Clan Histories of the Hopi (Forgotten Books, 2008) and Harold Courlander, *The Fourth World of the Hopis: The Epic Story of the Hopi Indians Preserved in their Legends and Traditions* (Albuquerque: University of New Mexico Press, 1987).
3. At the core of Hopi theology are the spirits commonly called *kachinas*. This work is by a Hopi person on that subject: Alph Secakuku, *Hopi Kachina Tradition: Following the Sun and Moon* (Outling: Northland, 1995).
4. For an overview of the Pueblo Revolt there is this Kindle edition available: David Roberts, *The Pueblo Revolt: The Secret Rebellion That Drove The Spaniards Out Of The Southwest* (New York: Simon and Schuster, 2008).
5. The religious oppression of the Hopi that led to the imprisonment of 19 Hopi parents is clearly summarized in this National Park Service online article, "Hopi Prisoners on the Rock" by Wendy Holliday: http://www.nps.gov/alca/historyculture/hopi-prisoners-on-the-rock.htm

8 The Garden

1. Neihardt, *Black Elk Speaks*, 74.
2. As I suggest in this chapter, the subject of sacrifice in world religion is vast and complex. For an overview try this study: Jeffrey Carter, ed., *Understanding Religious Sacrifice: A Reader* (London: Bloomsbury Academic, 2003).
3. The causes for and conduct of persecution in the early Christian church is a broad topic, but here is a primary source: William H.C. Frend, *Martyrdom and Persecution in the Early Church* (Cambridge: James Clarke & Company, 2008).
4. All Native traditions honored sacred land, but here is an illustrative example from the Navajo nation: Robert S. McPherson, *Sacred Land, Sacred View: Navajo Perceptions of the Four Corners Region* (Boulder: University Press of Colorado, 1992).
5. Matthew 26:38.
6. Like almost all speeches by historical Native American figures from the eighteenth and nineteenth centuries, this one by Tecumseh is often found with different variations. I chose this one from a simple online source because of its clarity to the point of Native attitudes toward death: http://www.indigenouspeople.net/tecumseh.htm
7. A good summary of the execution of thirty-eight Native men in 1862 can be found in an article online in The Nation, "Largest Mass Execution In US History: 150 Years Ago Today," by Jon Weiner published on December 26, 2012.: http://www.thenation.com/blog/171920/largest-mass-execution-us-history-150-years-ago-today#
8. Although there are many sources for a re-telling of the story of the White Buffalo Calf Woman, I was surprised to find one of the most simple and articulate on Wikipedia: http://en.wikipedia.org/wiki/White_Buffalo_Calf_Woman

9 The Cross

1. For a fresh look at the old story of Pocahontas, see: Linwood Custalow and Angela L. Daniel, *The True Story of Pochahontas* (Golden: Fulcrum Publishing, 2007).

2. To see the painting and learn more about its placement in the Capitol, the Architect of the Capitol resource online offers a clear image of the original: http://www.aoc.gov/capitol-hill/historic-rotunda-paintings/baptism-pocahontas

3. In this chapter I try to speak *to* historical issues of Native American women, but I make no pretense to speak *for* them. I will stand aside respectfully and allow my sisters to speak for themselves. But here is one resource for those who may not be familiar with that distinct voice in Native America: Carolyn Ross Johnston, *Voices of Cherokee Women* (Winston-Salem: John F. Blair, 2013).

4. The debate over the word "squaw" is as intense as it is for any other racially-charged terminology, which is why I believe we need to confront it. As for its original meaning and derivation, I found this curious, but informative resource online: http://anthropology.si.edu/goddard/squaw_1.pdf

5. Sexual violence against Indigenous women in the USA is widespread. According to US government statistics, Native American and Alaska Native women are more than 2.5 times more likely to be raped or sexually assaulted than other women in the USA. Some Indigenous women interviewed by Amnesty International said they didn't know anyone in their community who had not experienced sexual violence. Though rape is always an act of violence, there is evidence that Indigenous women are more likely than other women to suffer additional violence at the hands of their attackers. According to the US Department of Justice, in at least 86 per cent of the reported cases of rape or sexual assault against American Indian and Alaska Native women, survivors report that the perpetrators are non-Native men.

6. The term "Two-Spirit" is one that must be approached with care. In this chapter, I use it in a specific theological context to indicate the radically inclusive nature of Christ. However, it can and does have many nuanced meanings in both historic and contemporary Native society. One example of a source to uncover these issues is: Will Roscoe, *Changing Ones: Third and Fourth Genders in Native North America* (London: St. Martin's Griffin, 1998).

7. Galatians 3:28.

8. Matthew 27:39–40.

9. Matthew 27:41–43.

10. Matthew 27:44.

11. The term, "hoop of the nation," is an expression that refers to the unity of the people or community in Native America.

12. Matthew 27:53.

13. Luke 23:47.

14. Matthew 25:45.